Reading Esse[ntials]
and Note-Taking [Guide]
STUDENT WORKBOOK

Glencoe

ECONOMICS
Principles and Practices

With Features From
BusinessWeek
STANDARD
&POOR'S

McGraw Hill | **Glencoe**

New York, New York   Columbus, Ohio   Chicago, Illinois   Woodland Hills, California

To the Student

Economics: Principles and Practices **Reading Essentials and Note-Taking Guide** is designed to help you use recognized reading strategies to improve your reading-for-information skills. For each section of the student textbook, you are alerted to key content. Then, you are asked to draw from prior knowledge, organize your thoughts with a graphic organizer, and follow a process to read and understand the text. The **Reading Essentials and Note-Taking Guide** was prepared to help you get more from your textbook by reading with a purpose.

 Glencoe

The *McGraw·Hill* Companies

Send all inquiries to:
Glencoe/McGraw-Hill
8787 Orion Place
Columbus, OH 43240-4027

ISBN: 978-0-07-878593-1
MHID: 0-07-878593-6

Printed in the United States of America
4 5 6 7 8 9 10   009   10 09 08

Table of Contents

Scarcity and the Science of Economics

Big Idea

As you read pages 5–10 in your textbook, complete the graphic organizer below by listing and describing the three economic choices every society must make.

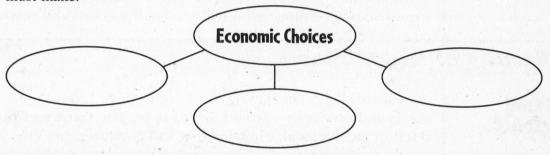

Economic Choices

Notes

Read to Learn

The Fundamental Economic Problem (page 6)

Analyzing Information

Label the following items as needs, wants, or resources.

1. Shelter

_____

2. Designer clothing

_____

3. Time

_____

4. Groceries

_____

5. Gas

_____

Scarcity is the basic economic problem of how to meet people's seemingly unlimited wants with scarce resources. This basic problem affects almost every economic decision people make as buyers and as sellers. Consider how people seem to always want more than they have. People's wants are unlimited but societies' resources are limited. **Economics** is the social science that studies how people satisfy seemingly unlimited and competing wants with the careful use of scarce resources.

When economists talk about people's unlimited wants, they are making a distinction between what people want and what they need. In economics, a **want** is something we would like to have but that is not necessary for survival, like a specific sneaker or particular type of house. A **need,** on the other hand, is a basic requirement for survival, such as food, clothing, and shelter.

Since all resources are limited, everything that meets a need or a want has a cost. Even when it seems as if something is "free," someone has to pay to produce it. That cost is ultimately passed on to consumers. Economists use the term **TINSTAAFL** to describe this concept. It means There Is No Such Thing As A Free Lunch.

Three Basic Questions (page 7)

Evaluating Information

When might a society choose to spend more money on social services versus defending itself?

_____

_____

The problem of scarcity forces every society to answer the basic questions of what, how, and for whom to produce. A society cannot produce everything its members want because it has limited resources. Societies must make decisions about what kinds of goods and services to produce and provide. For example, societies assess how to defend themselves and how to take care of people with disabilities. In addition, societies have to consider how to produce goods and services. Sometimes it may be more important to create jobs. Other times it may be more important to produce goods as cheaply as possible. Lastly, a society must determine who will receive the goods and services.

The Factors of Production (page 8)

Making Inferences

Why do some businesses disagree about environmental issues?

_____

_____

Factors of production are the resources used to make the goods and services we would like to have. **The factors of production** include land, capital, labor, and entrepreneurs.

In economics, **land** refers to natural resources or other "gifts of nature" not created by human effort. Land consists of oil, gold, sun, rain, animals, fish, rivers, and pastures. **Capital,** or **capital goods,** are the second factor of production. Capital goods are the tools, equipment, and factories used in the production of goods and services. A third factor of production is **labor,** or people with all their efforts, abilities, and skills. Entrepreneurs are special laborers—risk-taking individuals in search of profits. **Entrepreneurs** start new businesses or bring new products to the market.

The Scope of Economics (page 9)

Drawing Conclusions

Why is explanation a key element of economics?

_____

_____

The four key elements of the subject of economics are description, analysis, explanation, and prediction. We describe economic activity, including jobs, prices, and government spending, to know what the world looks like. **Gross Domestic Product (GDP)** is a statistic that describes the economic health of nations. GDP refers to the dollar value of all final goods, services, and structures produced within a country's borders during a one-year period. Another element of economics is the analysis of a described activity. The purpose of analysis is to discover why things work and how things happen. A third element of economics is explanation, or communication of knowledge. A fourth element of economics predicts what may happen in the future, based on the analysis of what is happening and what tends to happen.

Section Wrap-up

Answer these questions to check your understanding of the entire section.

1. Why is it important to distinguish between needs and wants?

_____

_____

_____

2. Why is economics a relevant subject for many people to study?

_____

_____

_____

Informative Writing

From the perspective of a municipal employee in your community, write a memo explaining a new initiative to develop an abandoned building for a specific community project, such as a recreation center, school, arts center, or public housing. Discuss what, how, and for whom the project will be produced.

_____

_____

_____

_____

_____

_____

_____

_____

_____

_____

_____

Basic Economic Concepts

Big Idea

As you read pages 12–17 in your textbook, complete the graphic organizer below by describing the factors that lead to economic growth.

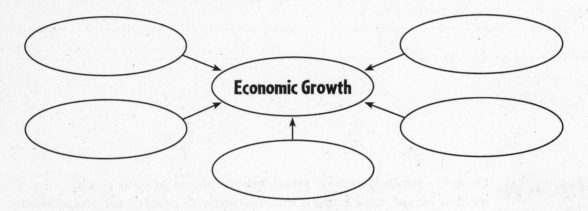

Notes | Read to Learn

Goods, Services, and Consumers (page 13)

Analyzing Information

List one good and one service provided by the following types of businesses:

Restaurant Good:

_____

Service:

_____

Car dealership Good:

_____

Service:

_____

Economic products command a price and satisfy wants and needs. Economic products include goods and services. A **good** is a tangible economic product that is useful, relatively scarce, and transferable to others. Examples of goods include books, bicycles, and computers. There are many types of goods. A capital good is a good producers use to make other goods and services, such as a machine in a factory. A **consumer good,** on the other hand, is intended for final use by consumers rather than businesses. Consumers are the people who use, or consume, goods and services to satisfy their wants and needs.

Goods can be further grouped into two categories: durable and nondurable. A **durable good** lasts for at least three years when used regularly. Durable goods can include capital goods and consumer goods. A **nondurable good** is a good that lasts for fewer than three years when used regularly. Food and clothing are examples of nondurable goods.

Unlike a good, a **service** is an item that cannot be touched. A service is work or labor performed for someone else, such as the work performed by engineers, plumbers, or entertainers.

 **Notes** | **Read to Learn**

Value, Utility, and Wealth (page 14)

Making Inferences

What would happen to the value of water if pollution or drought made it more scarce?

_____

Some goods and services are more valuable than others. **Value** describes the monetary worth of a good or service as determined by the market. The **paradox of value** refers to the contradiction between the high value of some nonessential items and the low value of some essential items. For a good or service to have value, it must be scarce and have **utility.** Utility is a product's ability to be useful and to provide satisfaction. People evaluate the utility of a particular good or service differently. When people or nations have a large number of valuable and tangible economic goods, they have **wealth.**

The Circular Flow of Economic Activity (page 15)

Determining Cause and Effect

How does a high unemployment rate affect the activity of product markets?

_____

_____

_____

The exchange of goods and services between consumers and businesses forms a circle. In economics, a **market** is any meeting place or mechanism that allows buyers and sellers to make an exchange. Individuals begin the circle in **factor markets,** or markets where the factors of production are bought and sold. There individuals earn income by selling their labor to businesses in the factor market. After individuals receive wages or salaries, they spend it in the **product markets,** or markets where goods and services are bought and sold. Businesses complete the circle when they use the funds generated by sales to produce more goods and services.

Productivity and Economic Growth (page 16)

Problems and Solutions

Describe one strategy governments use to increase productivity.

_____

_____

_____

Economic growth is an increase in a nation's total output of goods and services over time. The most important influence of economic growth is **productivity.** Productivity is the measure of the amount of output of goods and services in a specific period of time. Productivity increases whenever more goods and services are produced with the same amount of resources. It is an increase in the circular economic flow. Education, **division of labor,** and **specialization** all improve productivity by increasing **human capital.** Division of labor is how firms divide work into a number of separate tasks to be performed by different workers. Specialization is how firms assign tasks to the workers, factors, regions, or nations that can perform them more efficiently. The U.S. economy's high degree of **economic interdependence** is a result of specialization. Different countries specialize in different types of work. The U.S. relies on other countries, and in turn other countries rely on us, for goods and services to consume.

Section Wrap-up

Answer these questions to check your understanding of the entire section.

1. Use the terms scarcity and utility to explain the paradox of value.

_____

_____

_____

2. How does an increase in productivity increase the size of the circular flow of goods?

_____

_____

_____

Informative Writing

Write an essay that explains in what ways the United States invests in human capital. Also describe who pays for it and who benefits from it.

_____

_____

_____

_____

_____

_____

_____

_____

_____

_____

_____

_____

_____

Economic Choices and Decision Making

Big Idea

As you read pages 19–25 in your textbook, complete the graphic organizer below by identifying the ways in which you can make economic choices and what these strategies allow you to learn.

Problems	Strategy	Purpose
trade-offs	decision-making grid	

Notes

Read to Learn

Trade-Offs and Opportunity Cost *(page 20)*

Synthesizing Information

Why is the opportunity cost of a decision always less than the cost of the chosen good or service?

_____

_____

_____

Economists study how people make choices to satisfy their wants and needs with scarce resources. When people make choices, they consider their options. Every decision has trade-offs. A **trade-off** is an alternative that is available whenever a choice is to be made. People can use a decision-making grid to systematically analyze alternatives when they make an economic decision. Decision-making grids show a number of alternatives and the criteria used to analyze the alternatives. For example, a decision-making grid could compare colleges based on the criteria of location, price, and expertise in a particular subject.

When economists evaluate the cost of a good or service, they consider more than just the price. They also consider the **opportunity cost,** or the cost of the next-best alternative use of money, time, or resources. For example, the opportunity cost of going to the mall on a Sunday may be not watching a football game on TV.

Production Possibilities (page 21)

Making Inferences

How does a production possibilities frontier change if the economy declines?

_____

_____

_____

Another way to analyze economic choices is by plotting the possible production of two products on a graph called the **production possibilities frontier.** This graph represents the maximum combinations of goods and/or services an economy can produce when using all productive resources. All points on the production possibilities frontier show the maximum potential output at a given point in time. Output values to the right, or outside of the curve, cannot be reached without additional resources. Reaching only an output value to the left, or inside the curve, would indicate that resources are not being fully used or methods of production are inefficient. The production possibilities frontier shows the opportunity cost of making more of one good or service versus another. Economic growth is the result of more resources or greater productivity. This causes the curve to move outward, both up and to the right.

Thinking Like an Economist (page 23)

Analyzing Information

Explain why economic models are simplified?

_____

_____

Economists can analyze choices by using economic models, such as the production possibilities frontier, or by using a **cost-benefit analysis.** An **economic model** is a simplified version of a complex concept or behavior expressed in the form of an equation, graph, or illustration. Economists create models based on assumptions, or factors they decide are true or constant. A cost-benefit analysis helps people make decisions by comparing the cost of an action to its benefits. A decision-making grid is one example of a cost-benefit analysis.

The Road Ahead (page 24)

Making Generalizations

How can the finding from economic analysis positively affect the standard of living?

_____

_____

_____

You can apply economic concepts to your daily life. Learning about economics will help you to become a better citizen, as most solutions to political problems involve economics. Economics describes how things are made, bought, sold, and used. Economic models and tools, such as cost-benefit analysis, aid decisions made by all market participants.

In addition, economics helps explain the workings of a **free enterprise economy.** This economic system is a market economy in which privately owned businesses have the freedom to operate for profit with limited government intervention. In other kinds of economic systems, governments and consumers make economic decisions differently. All economic topics explain in some way people's **standard of living,** or quality of life.

Section Wrap-up

Answer these questions to check your understanding of the entire section.

1. How is opportunity cost shown on a production possibilities frontier?

_____

_____

_____

2. Which market participants might use a cost-benefit analysis to make economic decision?

_____

_____

_____

Informative Writing

Write an e-mail to a friend using cost-benefit analysis to help him or her decide whether to accept an offer for a high-paying job in a big city across the country or to accept an offer for a lower-paying job in his or her hometown.

_____

_____

_____

_____

_____

_____

_____

_____

_____

_____

_____

_____

_____

Economic Systems

Big Idea

As you read pages 33–41 in your textbook, complete this graphic organizer by filling in the ways in which a market economy differs from, and is similar to, a command economy.

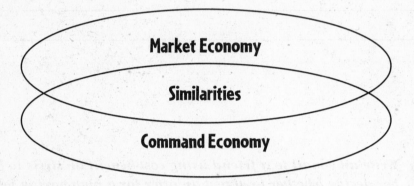

Market Economy

Similarities

Command Economy

 **Notes** | **Read to Learn**

Traditional Economies *(page 34)*

Determining Cause and Effect

How does living in a traditional economy affect the role of the individual?

_____

_____

_____

_____

_____

An **economic system** is how a nation uses its resources to satisfy its people's needs and wants in an organized way. In fact, the way a society organizes itself determines that society's economic system. There are three major types of economic systems: traditional, command, and market. However, in the real world, almost all economies are a mixture of these three types.

In a **traditional economy,** the use of scarce resources is based on ritual, habit, or custom. In effect, the entire society is based on handed-down ways of living. The role of an individual in such a society is based on custom, not that individual's desires. For example, if your parents were hunters, you would become a hunter, as well. You would also hunt and distribute the rewards of your hunt the same way as your parents. The advantages of a traditional economy are that everyone knows what, how, and for whom to produce. The main disadvantage is that both new ideas and new ways of doing things are not encouraged. Traditional societies usually punish people who act differently. As a result, a lack of innovation leads to economic stagnation and a lower standard of living than other economic systems.

Command Economies (page 35)

Making Inferences

As you read, complete the sentence below:

A command economy does not encourage _____.

In a **command economy,** a central authority (usually the government) makes all major economic decisions. The government also restricts property rights and gives individuals little freedom. The main advantage of a command economy is that it can change the direction of economic production in major ways. The disadvantages of a command economy are that it ignores the wants and needs of consumers; encourages people to fill a quota instead of making a good product; requires a large, slow, and expensive bureaucracy; lacks flexibility to address changing needs; and lacks rewards for individual initiative.

Market Economies (page 37)

Analyzing Information

How does competition lead to economic uncertainty?

_____

_____

In a **market economy,** consumers and businesses have the freedom to make economic decisions in their best interests. A **market** is a place or method where buyers and sellers come together to exchange goods and services. Market economies are often called **capitalism**—an economic system in which individuals own the factors of production and decide their use.

The advantages of market economies include a great deal of individual freedom, gradual adjustment to change over time, less government interference, decentralized decision-making, the production of a variety of goods and services, and greater consumer satisfaction. The disadvantages are the inability to provide goods and services for everyone, inadequate provision of some basic goods and services, and a high degree of uncertainty due to competition.

Mixed Economies (page 39)

Comparing and Contrasting

As you read, complete the sentence below:

Socialism allows some

_____

ownership, but communism has none.

Most countries have a **mixed economy.** Norway's economy is a mix of capitalism and socialism. **Socialism** is a mixed system in which the government owns some of the factors of production and also provides some of its people's basic needs.

North Korea's economy is based solely on communism. **Communism** is a more strict form of socialism, in which the factors of production are owned collectively and controlled by the state.

An advantage of a mixed economy is that it can provide for those in society who might be left out, such as children, the elderly, and the disabled. Its disadvantages include expensive services, in some socialist countries limited availability or deterioration in the quality of services over time, socialism and communism are inefficient when compared to capitalism.

Section Wrap-up

Answer these questions to check your understanding of the entire section.

1. Why does a command economy require a large bureaucracy?

_____

_____

_____

2. Why might a democratic political system result in a market economy?

_____

_____

_____

Informative Writing

Explain how a market economy works by writing a news story about the rise in popularity of a particular good or service. The story should show how the freedoms of both the business and the consumer affected the success of the good or service. Remember to tell when, where, who, and how the events took place.

_____

_____

_____

_____

_____

_____

_____

_____

_____

_____

_____

_____

Evaluating Economic Performance

Big Idea

As you read pages 43–46 in your textbook, complete this graphic organizer by filling in the seven major economic and social goals of Americans.

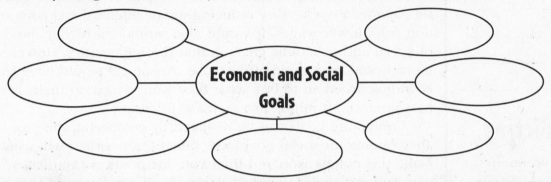

Economic and Social Goals

 **Notes**

Read to Learn

Economic and Social Goals *(page 44)*

Analyzing Information

For each goal below name a part of American culture or history that represents it, such as a phrase on money or from the Constitution.

1. *Economic freedom*

_____

2. *Economic equity*

_____

3. *Economic security*

_____

Americans share several major economic and social goals. One goal is *economic freedom*. Its purpose is to allow individuals to make their own economic decisions, including choosing occupations and choosing how to spend and produce. *Economic efficiency* is another shared goal. Resources are scarce and producers must use the factors of production wisely. Americans believe that equal work should receive equal pay, which is *economic equity*. For example, there is a national **minimum wage**—the lowest wage that employers legally can pay.

Americans also want protection from losing their jobs because of events outside of their control, so *economic security* is also a goal. The government created **Social Security** to provide retirement and disability benefits for workers.

Most people need jobs to support themselves. Thus, *full employment* is another shared goal. The problem of **inflation**—a general rise in prices—makes *price stability* a goal, especially for people who live on a **fixed income**—an income that does not increase as prices go up. The final goal is *economic growth,* which allows most people to have more goods and services.

Resolving Trade-Offs Among Goals *(page 46)*

Formulating Questions

Before you read this passage, write two questions that will help you organize your notes.

1. _____

_____

2. _____

_____

Predicting

1. What economic goals would be considered to decide whether or not to limit the federal budget deficit?

_____

_____

_____

2. What are the opportunity costs involved in either decision?

_____

_____

_____

People differ in their opinions about how to reach a particular economic or social goal. Sometimes, the goals themselves are in conflict. Therefore, a society must consider the opportunity costs of its conflicting economic and social policies when it makes economic decisions.

For example, if Americans do not approve of a country's child labor practices, the government may decide to keep certain clothing items made in that country out of the United States. This decision would further the goal of economic equity for American workers by reducing unfair international competition from lower wages. It would also promote a higher standard of social and economic goals in that foreign country. However, there would be a trade-off because consumers would have less economic freedom to buy what they want based on their own best interests. It might also increase prices.

Conflicting goals can be resolved by comparing the cost of an economic or social goal to its benefit. Americans will usually make this comparison and then vote for political candidates who support their individual decisions. If a majority of voters think that they are paying too much for particular goods, then trade restrictions might be lifted. That would increase supply and competition, resulting in lower prices. The trade restrictions might stay lifted until unemployment rises. Then a majority of voters might believe that imports should be restricted again.

In the United States, people, businesses, and government are usually able to resolve conflicts among goals. The American economic system is flexible. It allows for choices and accommodates compromise while satisfying most people.

Our economic and social goals will change as the goals of the American people change. In a democracy, the government and its laws reflect the will of the people. Programs such as Social Security or Medicare, as well as laws that provide unemployment insurance and set a minimum wage, show how much Americans have changed their free enterprise economy over time, and how they will continue to do so.

Section Wrap-up

Answer these questions to check your understanding of the entire section.

1. Why is economic security such an important goal to Americans?

_____

_____

_____

2. Have Americans always shared the same social and economic goals throughout history? Explain.

_____

_____

_____

Expository Writing

Which economic and social goals do you think are most important? Use the graphic organizer you completed on page 13 of this section to help you choose three goals and to organize an essay that defines them. In your essay, remember to explain why you chose the three goals.

_____

_____

_____

_____

_____

_____

_____

_____

_____

_____

American Free Enterprise

Big Idea

As you read pages 48–53 in your textbook, complete this graphic organizer by filling in the five major economic and social goals of Americans.

Characteristic	Example

 **Notes**

Read to Learn

Characteristics of Free Enterprise Capitalism *(page 49)*

Making Generalizations

As you read, complete the sentence below:

The characteristics of free enterprise depend on a political system that protects

_____.

America's economy is based on a capitalistic **free-enterprise system.** Individuals are *free* to own resources and decide how to use them. Ample competition exists because there is minimal government interference. There are five main characteristics of capitalism. The first is **economic freedom.** Individuals are free to choose what to buy and how to earn an income. Businesses are free to make their own business decisions in regards to who to hire, what to produce, how much to produce, where to sell it, and what to charge for it. The second characteristic is that buyers and sellers freely and willingly engage in market transactions. This is called **voluntary exchange. Private property rights** are another important feature of capitalism because they allow people to freely own and control property. Such rights give people the incentive to work, save, and invest. **Profit motive** is the fourth characteristic of capitalism. The desire to earn a profit drives people to take risks in the hope of improving their well-being. The profit motive stimulates growth in a free-enterprise system. Finally, **competition**—the struggle among sellers to attract consumers—is also a characteristic of capitalism.

 **Notes** | **Read to Learn**

The Role of the Entrepreneur (page 50)

Predicting

What will happen if there is low demand for an entrepreneur's good or service?

_____

_____

_____

Entrepreneurs are the driving force of the free enterprise system. They are the people who start new businesses that help the economy grow. Why do entrepreneurs take risks? The profit motive propels them. Entrepreneurs organize and manage land, capital, and labor in an effort to collect wealth or profit. Entrepreneurs want to be their own boss, and they are willing to risk failure to achieve their goals. Many entrepreneurs do fail. Others stay in business and reach various levels of success. Only a very few actually do become very wealthy. Everyone benefits from entrepreneurs' success. Workers have higher paying jobs; consumers have more choices, and the government earns higher tax receipts.

The Role of the Consumer (page 51)

Making Inferences

What is one way individuals can encourage businesses to make environmentally friendly products?

_____

_____

Consumers are the "kings and queens" of the free enterprise system. Their position of power is called **consumer sovereignty.** As consumers make purchases, they tell producers of goods and services what and how much to produce. When consumers are not satisfied with a particular good or service, they will buy a different one. Consumers' tastes, wants, and needs are constantly changing. For example, the wide spread use of the Internet resulted in millions of consumers purchasing goods and services online instead of going to retail stores. The producers who succeed in the marketplace are the ones who pay attention to consumers' "votes" for and against various goods and services.

The Role of Government (page 52)

Determining Cause and Effect

How does the government's roles as protector, provider, and regulator affect its role as consumer?

_____

_____

_____

American citizens have shown that they want the government to intervene in the economy. As a *protector,* the government passes and enforces laws. There are laws against selling unsafe products and against economic discrimination. As a *provider,* the government supplies goods and services, such as roads and policing. The government is also a regulator—it makes rules about how people and businesses may behave. Government preserves competition and oversees commercial transactions in the market. Finally, government is also a *consumer.* The U.S. government is the second largest spender in the economy.

Although Americans can buy, sell, and invest fairly freely, government intervention and regulation means that our economic system is actually a **mixed,** or **modified free enterprise economy.**

Section Wrap-up

Answer these questions to check your understanding of the entire section.

1. Explain how consumers benefit from economic freedom and voluntary exchange.

_____

_____

_____

2. How is the government's role in the American economy generally justified?

_____

_____

_____

Persuasive Writing

Think about a problem that the current economy in the United States might face today, such as high unemployment, low minimum wage, or failing educational system. Then write an essay that argues for or against more government intervention in the economy as a solution to the problem. Use evidence from this section to support your argument.

_____

_____

_____

_____

_____

_____

_____

_____

_____

_____

_____

_____

Forms of Business Organization

Big Idea

As you read pages 61–70 in your textbook, complete this graphic organizer to show how the three types of business organizations differ from one another.

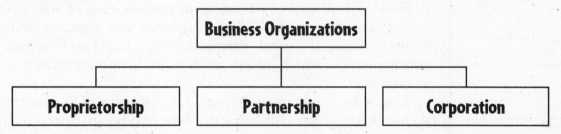

Business Organizations

Proprietorship   Partnership   Corporation

 **Notes**   **Read to Learn**

Sole Proprietorships *(page 62)*

Drawing Conclusions

How can a proprietorship still be profitable if that form of business represents the smallest percentage of the total sales?

_____

_____

_____

_____

_____

There are three main forms of business organization. The most common form is the **sole proprietorship,** in which a business is owned and run by a single individual. **Proprietorships** are the smallest form of business and have the smallest percentage of total sales, but they can still be profitable.

Proprietorships have several advantages. They are easy to start up, they are simple to manage, owners keep the profits without having to share with other owners, and they are easy to discontinue. Also, there are no business taxes to pay because proprietorships are not recognized as a legal entity. Many proprietors also enjoy being their own boss.

Proprietorships have significant disadvantages as well, including that the owner is personally responsible for all losses and debts of the business. This is called having **unlimited liability.** Other disadvantages include the difficulty of raising financial capital, and the difficulty of attracting qualified employees. Also, proprietorships have **limited life.** This means it is discontinued if the owner dies, quits, or sells the business. The business might also have to carry a minimum **inventory** in reserve for customers.

 **Notes**

Read to Learn

Partnerships (page 64)

Evaluating Information

Why would partners in a business draw up legal papers to specify arrangements between them?

_____

_____

_____

_____

_____

_____

Partnerships are another form of business. They are jointly owned by two or more persons. There are fewer partnerships than other forms of business, and they have the second smallest percentage of sales and net income. There are two kinds of partnerships: general and limited. **General partnerships** require all partners to be responsible for the management and financial obligations of the business. In **limited partnerships,** at least one partner is not active in running the business, and has limited responsibility for its debts. Legal papers often specify arrangements between the partners.

Some advantages of partnerships include ease of start up, ease of management, lack of special taxes, and a greater ability to obtain financial capital. Partnerships are larger in size than proprietorships, which allows them to enjoy more efficient operations.

The main disadvantage of general partnerships is that each partner is fully responsible for the acts of other partners. In limited partnerships, a partner's responsibility for business debts is limited by the amount of his or her investment. Both types of partnerships have a limited life and conflicts can occur.

Corporations (page 67)

Comparing and Contrasting

What is the difference between common stock and preferred stock?

_____

_____

Synthesizing Information

As you read, complete the sentence:

_____ *own corporations, but*

_____

run them.

Corporations are a form of business organization that is owned by many people. They comprise about one fifth of American businesses, but make a majority of all sales. To form a corporation, the federal or state government must grant a **charter.** It states the company's name, address, purpose, and the number of ownership certificates, or shares of **stocks.** Investors called **stockholders** (or **shareholders**) then own the corporation. If the corporation is successful, **dividends,** or payments of a small part of the profits, may be issued to the stockholders.

Two kinds of stocks that give stockholders ownership rights are common and preferred. **Common stock** gives owners one vote for each share of stock. Owners use their votes to select a board of directors to set policies. Owners of **preferred stock** cannot vote for board members; however, they receive dividends before common stockholders.

Corporations have advantages over other forms of businesses. They can borrow money easily by issuing bonds A **bond** is a written promise to repay the **principal,** or amount borrowed at a later date. The corporation pays **interest** to the lender. They are disadvantaged, however, because they are subject to government regulations and **double taxation** of profits.

Answer these questions to check your understanding of the entire section.

1. What is the easiest form of business to start up? What are its advantages?

_____

_____

_____

2. Explain two ways in which individuals can invest in corporations.

_____

_____

_____

Informative Writing

Many well-known businesses, such as Microsoft, Disney, and Ben and Jerry's, started out as partnerships and then formed corporations. Explain what factors would motivate a partnership to become a corporation.

_____

_____

_____

_____

_____

_____

_____

_____

_____

_____

_____

Business Growth and Expansion

Big Idea

As you read pages 72–77 in your textbook, complete the graphic organizer below by comparing a vertical merger to a horizontal merger.

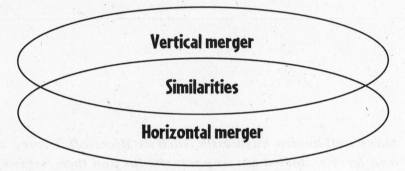

Vertical merger

Similarities

Horizontal merger

Notes	Read to Learn

Growth Through Reinvestment *(page 73)*

Analyzing Information

Which financial statement provides the most complete picture of a business' success? Explain:

_____

_____

_____

Most business managers rely on financial statements to keep track of how the business is doing. An **income statement** is a report that shows a business's sales, expenses, net income, and cash flow for a determined period of time.

Income statements show a business's **net income**—the funds left over after all of the business's expenses are subtracted from its sales. One of the most important business expenses is **depreciation.** It is a *noncash* charge for the wear and tear on a business's capital goods. Each year capital goods lose a portion of their value, so the value of the business's assets, or property, decreases each year. The money stays in the business's accounts. As a result, it is counted as income.

A business's **cash flow** represents its *bottom line*. Cash flow is the sum of net income and noncash charges, such as depreciation. If a business has a positive cash flow, the owners have several options. If the business is a corporation, it might pay or increase dividends. The owners of a proprietorship or partnership might pay themselves. Any type of business can reinvest its revenue back into the business, so it can grow.

 **Notes** | **Read to Learn**

Growth Through Mergers (page 74)

Growth Through Mergers (page 74)

Problems and Solutions

Suppose a drug company sells a product that harms a large number of consumers. The problem receives widespread attention in the media. What is one of their options?

_____

_____

_____

_____

Synthesizing Information

What factors would a nation consider in deciding whether to allow a multinational to locate within its borders?

_____

_____

_____

_____

_____

_____

One way that businesses can expand is by engaging in a **merger**. A merger occurs when two or more businesses combine to form a single firm. Viacom has grown through many horizontal and vertical mergers. A **horizontal merger** is when businesses that produce the same kind of product combine. Viacom first grew by buying other cable televisions systems. Later, Viacom purchased MTV networks which included cable television channels. This is an example of a **vertical merger.** A vertical merger is when businesses involved in different stages of manufacturing or marketing merge. Viacom merged with cable television channels which produced or owned programming. Through merging with many other firms, Viacom has become one of the largest media corporations.

Mergers occur for a variety of reasons. Businesses merge to grow faster, to become more efficient, to acquire or deliver a better product, to eliminate a rival, or to change its image. For example, some businesses cannot grow as quickly as they would like using funds generated internally. A merger helps them to grow more quickly. Other businesses merge to increase efficiency. A merger allows the new firm to eliminate redundant jobs, make more efficient use of its advertising, and take advantage of volume discounts.

Firms benefits from mergers in other ways. Mergers can allow a firm to quickly acquire new technology and product lines. Two businesses can join forces to quickly catch up with, or even eliminate, rivals. A business can also use a merger to lose its corporate identity. This is useful when a particular business has negative publicity, such as a scandal.

Some corporations become so large through mergers and acquisitions that it turns into a **conglomerate,** or a corporation comprised of at least four businesses. Each business must make unrelated products and not be responsible for a majority of its sales. Corporations commonly become conglomerates to allow for diversification. In other words, if one part of a conglomerate is not doing well, the other parts may not be affected.

Some large corporations have become multinationals. A **multinational** is a corporation that has manufacturing or service operations in a number of countries. These firms are usually welcome because they transfer new technology and create jobs. They also produce tax revenues for the host country. However, some multinationals have been criticized for paying low wages, exporting natural resources, or interfering with the development of local business. Generally, however, the advantages of multinationals outweigh the disadvantages.

Section Wrap-up

Answer these questions to check your understanding of the entire section.

1. Why is a cash flow statement a key type of financial statement?

_____

_____

_____

2. What is the difference between a conglomerate and a multinational?

_____

_____

_____

Informative Writing

Did you know that Pepsico owns the brands Gatorade, Tropicana, Frito-Lay, and Quaker? Describe what kind of merger this combination of brands represents and in what ways all the companies benefit.

_____

_____

_____

_____

_____

_____

_____

_____

_____

_____

_____

Nonprofit Organizations

Big Idea

As you read pages 79–83 in your textbook, complete the graphic organizer below by describing the benefits of nonprofit organizations.

Organization	Benefits
Community organization	
Consumer cooperative	

Notes

Read to Learn

Community Organizations and Cooperatives (page 80)

Making Inferences

In what ways would a nonprofit work like a business?

_____

_____

_____

_____

_____

A **nonprofit organization** works like a business to promote the interests of its members. Unlike the typical corporation, it does not seek profit for its owners.

Nonprofit community organizations include schools, churches, and hospitals. Many of these organizations are formed as corporations to take advantage of the corporate structure. They do not, however, issue stock, pay dividends, or pay income taxes. It is not easy to analyze the economic value of their work, but the large number of these organizations shows that they are important to our economic system.

A common type of nonprofit organization is the **cooperative, or co-op.** These are voluntary associations formed to carry on an economic activity that benefits its members. There are three main types of cooperatives: consumer, service, and producer. A *consumer cooperative* buys bulk amounts of goods on behalf of its members. Members keep costs down by devoting time to the operation. A *service cooperative* provides services (such as a **credit union**) to its members. A *producer cooperative* helps members promote or sell their products.

Labor, Professional, and Business Organizations *(page 81)*

Comparing and Contrasting

How is a chamber of commerce and a trade association similar to and different from each other?

Similar:

_____

_____

Different:

_____

_____

A **labor union** is a nonprofit organization of workers formed to protect its members' interests in employment matters. A union participates in **collective bargaining** when it negotiates with management about pay, working hours, and other job-related issues.

Other workers belong to nonprofit **professional associations.** These consist of people in specialized occupations who are interested in improving the working conditions, skills levels, and public perception of the profession.

Businesses organize to promote their collective interests as well. One example is a **chamber of commerce.** This type of organization promotes the welfare of its member businesses including lobbying laws that favor that particular type of business. Trade associations are another type of organization that is particularly interested in governments' policies which affect businesses. They represent specific kinds of businesses and are mindful of such issues as free enterprise and imports and tariffs.

Some business associations are devoted to protecting consumers. The **Better Business Bureau** keeps records about consumer inquiries and complaints about local businesses.

Government *(page 82)*

Drawing Conclusions

As you read, complete the sentence below:

Businesses with few competitors can _____ prices which is one reason that the government regulates public utilities.

Local, state, and national governments are also nonprofit economic organizations. Many governments produce and distribute goods and services. As a result, governments have a direct role in the economy. Many government organizations, such as the U.S. Postal Service, are government-owned corporations. Like privately owned businesses, these corporations have a board of directors that hires professional managers to oversee daily operations. Like for-profit corporations, these organizations charge for their products and services.

Government also plays an indirect role in the economy. It does so when it acts as a regulator to help the market economy operate smoothly and efficiently. One example is the regulation of **public utilities,** municipal or investor-owned companies that offer products such as water, sewerage, and electric services. These types of firms often have few competitors, so consumers want the government to supervision them.

The government also plays an indirect role when it grants money to people in the form of Social Security checks and other benefits. How citizens use these funds influences the production of goods and services. This in turn affects how scarce resources are allocated.

Answer these questions to check your understanding of the entire section.

1. How are nonprofit organizations different from corporations?

_____

_____

_____

2. Describe one direct way and one indirect way in which the government is involved in the economy.

_____

_____

_____

Informative Writing

Think of a need in your community that would be best met by a non-profit organization. Write a letter explaining your community's need, the form of the organization, how you will create it, and why you believe it will meet that need.

_____

_____

_____

_____

_____

_____

_____

_____

_____

_____

_____

_____

What is Demand?

Big Idea

As you read pages 91–95 in your textbook, complete this graphic organizer by filling in the ovals below with the characteristics of demand.

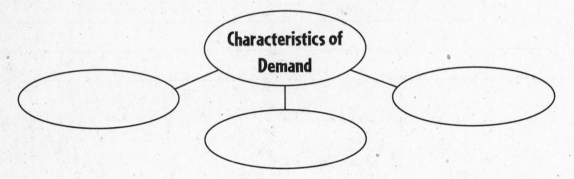

Characteristics of Demand

 **Notes** | **Read to Learn**

An Introduction to Demand (page 92)

Drawing Conclusions

As you read, complete the sentence below:

Businesses can use a demand curve to determine at what _____ they should sell their product.

In a **market economy,** people and businesses make economic decisions based on their own interests. **Microeconomics** is the study of small units or small factors of an economy.

When businesses or individuals have the desire, ability, and willingness to buy a product, they create **demand** for that product. Both the price and the amount of a certain good or service demanded at a specific time determine overall demand.

There are two ways economists analyze demand. One way is to use a table called a **demand schedule.** The table consists of two columns: one shows the prices for a good or service and the second column shows the quantity demanded for the good or service at each price. When economists plot the data from a demand schedule onto a graph, they have a **demand curve.** A demand curve shows the quantity of a good or product a consumer demands at every possible price. The price is on the left side (vertical axis) of the graph and the quantity is on the bottom (horizontal axis) of the graph. The demand curve is the line formed by connecting the data points on the graph. The demand curve always slopes downward from left to right.

The Law of Demand (page 93)

Before you read about the Law of Demand, write two questions that you hope the passage will answer.

1. _____
_____
_____

2. _____
_____
_____
_____

Both a demand schedule and a demand curve show the relationship between price and quantity demand. Note that the demand schedule and the demand curve shows how the price of a good or service increases as the quantity demanded decreases. The opposite is also true. When the price of a good or service decreases, the quantity demanded increases. This is called the Law of Demand. The **Law of Demand** is a rule that states consumers will buy more of a product at a lower price and less of a product at a higher price. You can observe the Law of Demand the next time your local mall has a sale. You will see that people will buy more items when prices go down.

Sometimes businesses want to know the whole market's demand for a particular item instead of one person's demand. In order to study the market's demand, they plot a graph of the **market demand curve** for a particular product. It shows the quantity of the item everyone in the market is able and willing to buy at each possible price. The market demand curve is the line on a graph representing the sum of the quantities demanded by all buyers at each possible price.

Demand and Marginal Utility (page 95)

Making Generalizations

As you read, complete the sentence below:

Because of diminishing marginal utility businesses can expect the demand of a product to _____ over time if both the _____ and _____ stay the same.

Factors, such as *utility,* affects demand. Utility is the satisfaction consumers receive from a product. When consumers buy more than one of the same item, they receive additional satisfaction or usefulness from buying additional units of the product. The additional satisfaction is called **marginal utility.** As consumers buy more units of a product, however, the additional satisfaction they receive from each purchase decreases. Economists call this **diminishing marginal utility.**

Both marginal utility and diminishing marginal utility affect demand. Although consumers might purchase one more of the same item, they might not be willing to buy two or even three more units of the same product at the same price. For example, suppose Kellogg's creates a new type of cereal called "Banana Coconut Flakes." The first box that you buy, you enjoy a lot. You like the flavor and you like a change in your daily routine. You will not enjoy the second box as much. It is not new to you and maybe you notice that it becomes soggy too quickly in milk. When you consider buying a third box, you notice it is more expensive than other cereals. At this point, you will probably decide that "Banana Coconut Flakes" is not worth the extra money and buy a cheaper cereal instead.

Section Wrap-up

Answer these questions to check your understanding of the entire section.

1. How might one business's decision to sell goods at a price lower than its competitors impact the economy?

_____

_____

_____

2. Why is the Law of Demand an important rule of economics?

_____

_____

_____

Expository Writing

Suppose you just put a new type of sneaker on the market. Your new sneaker faces many competitors, but the initial demand is very high. Describe the steps you will take to keep the quantity demanded of your sneakers the same over time.

_____

_____

_____

_____

_____

_____

_____

_____

_____

_____

_____

_____

Factors Affecting Demand

Big Idea

As you read pages 97–101 in your textbook, complete this graphic organizer by filling in the determinants of demand, an example of each, and how each affects demand.

Determinants of Demand		
Determinant	**Example**	**Effect on demand**

 **Notes**

Read to Learn

Change in the Quantity Demanded (page 98)

Synthesizing Information

As you read, complete the sentence below:

When the price of one product increases, in comparison, the price of its substitutes seems to _____.

A **change in quantity demanded** is a movement from one point to another along the demand curve. In fact, the amount of a good or service a consumer is willing and able to buy changes when its price changes. For example, a consumer will buy one DVD for $25. If the price drops to $19, a point further to the right on the demand curve, a consumer will buy three DVDs. In order to further understand this principle, we can look at the income effect and substitution effect.

The **income effect** is a change in quantity demanded caused by a change in consumers' real income when a price changes. When the price of an item decreases, consumers feel a little "richer" because they spent less money than they expected. Conversely, when the price of an item increases, consumers feel a little "poorer" because they have spent more money than they expected. The **substitution effect** is a change in quantity demanded caused by a change in price that makes alternate products more or less expensive. For example, if the price of DVDs decreased significantly, families would choose to buy more DVDs instead of going to the movies—a more expensive substitute.

Change in Demand *(page 99)*

Underline the sentence that clarifies the difference between the representation of a change in demand and a change in quantity demanded.

Predicting

As you read, complete the following sentence:

1. If the price of gasoline rises and affects consumer tastes, the market demand curve for fuel-efficient cars will

_____ .

2. If Nintendo announced that in six months it was going to release a new and improved video game system, how would the demand for the current video game system be affected?

_____

_____

_____

What happens when the price of a good or service stays the same but other factors change? People may decide to buy a *different* amount of the product at that same price. This is a **change in demand**—a shift of the whole demand curve to the right or the left. When the demand curve shifts to the left, there is an decrease in demand. When the demand curve shifts to the right, there is a increase in demand. When demand changes while price remains the same, the result is a new curve that shows the new quantity demanded at all possible prices. To summarize, a *change in demand* results in an entirely new demand curve, while a *change in quantity demanded* is a movement along the initial demand curve.

Change in demand can be caused by changes in the determinants of demand, such as consumer income, consumer tastes, the price of related goods, expectations, and the number of consumers. If consumer income changes, consumers will purchase different amounts of goods and services at all possible prices. For example, suppose taxpayers receive a tax refund. They could use the refund to buy more DVDs. Then, if you plotted the number of DVDs that would be bought at every possible price after a tax refund, the demand curve would be to the right of the previous one. If consumer income decreased, due to a tax increase for example, the demand curve for DVDs would be to the left of the initial demand curve.

Consumer tastes affect demand when consumers' opinions about particular products change. Many new products, particularly technology products, will have a higher demand than similar products that have been available for some time.

Demand can also change because of a change in the price of **complements** or **substitutes.** Substitutes are competing products that can be used in place of one another. For example, the demand for corn oil will increase if the price of canola oil, a substitute, increases and vice versa. Complements are products that affect demand because the use of one increases the use of the other. For example, DVD players and DVDs are complementary. When the price of DVD players fall, consumers buy more DVD players *and* more DVDs.

Consumer expectations and the number of consumers can also affect demand. For example, consumers may not buy a product if they expect that a better product will be put on the market or they might buy more if they believe there will be a future shortage of a product. Finally, a change in the number of consumers will affect the market demand curve as more or fewer consumers seek to purchase a particular good or service.

Section Wrap-up

Answer these questions to check your understanding of the entire section.

1. What does a movement along the demand curve show?

_____

_____

_____

2. Which determinants of demand could be affected by new technologies?

_____

_____

_____

Informative Writing

Suppose that you work for a fried-snack-food company. News channels have televised reports encouraging people to eat healthy snacks. Write a report to your manager that explains the recent decrease in sales and offer ways that the company can reverse this trend.

_____

_____

_____

_____

_____

_____

_____

_____

_____

_____

_____

Elasticity of Demand

Big Idea

As you read pages 103–109 in your textbook, complete this graphic organizer by filling in the effect a change in price has on quantity demanded if the demand curve is elastic, inelastic, or unit elastic.

Change in Price

Notes | Read to Learn

Demand Elasticity (page 104)

Synthesizing Information

A demand curve with a gradual slope downward from left to right is _____ *while a demand curve with a steep downward slope from left to right is* _____ .

Elasticity is an economic measure that shows how a dependant variable, such as quantity demanded, responds to a change of an independent variable, such as price. One kind of elasticity is **demand elasticity.** It can be elastic, inelastic, or unit elastic.

Demand is **elastic** when a change in price causes a significantly larger change in quantity demanded. This is when a demand curve shows a percentage change in quantity demanded that is greater than the percentage change in price. An elastic demand curve slopes gently downward from left to right. Fresh tomatoes are an example of a good that has elastic demand.

Demand is **inelastic** when a change in price causes a relatively small change in the quantity demanded. For example, if the price of toothpaste was half of its regular price, people would still buy just what they needed. As well, if the price was doubled, the demand would not change significantly either. The cost of toothpaste would still be a small part of a person's budget.

Demand is **unit elastic** when the percentage change in quantity demanded equals the percentage change in price.

The Total Expenditures Test (page 105)

Drawing Conclusions

After you read, underline the sentence in the second paragraph that supports the following conclusion:

A business owner who wants to increase revenue should not increase the price of a product that has an elastic demand.

A discussion of elasticity may seem very technical. However, elasticity is a very important concept for all businesses. Suppose a business wants to increase its revenue by raising prices. It could test elasticity first to see if demand for the product is elastic, inelastic, or unit elastic.

In order to determine elasticity, businesses use the total expenditures test. The test is a study of the impact of a price change on total expenditures, or how much consumers spend on a product at a particular price. Businesses find total expenditures by multiplying the price of a product by the quantity demanded. Then they test elasticity by observing the change in total expenditures between two points on the demand curve. When the demand curve is elastic, the relationship between the change in price and total expenditures is "inverse"—when the price goes down, total expenditures go up. When the demand curve is inelastic, total expenditures go down when the price goes down. When the demand curve is unit elastic, total expenditures remain unchanged when the price goes down.

Determinants of Demand Elasticity (page 107)

Making Generalizations

As you read, complete the following sentence:
The demand for luxury cars is

_____.

Write the answer for each question in the passage to support your generalization.

1. _____

2. _____

3. _____

Answers to the following three questions also help determine demand elasticity.

Can the purchase be delayed? The purchase of products like gold jewelry, with an elastic demand, can be delayed without hardship. But when a consumer cannot put off a purchase, such as electricity, it tends to make demand inelastic.

Are adequate substitutes available? If there are adequate substitutes, consumers can choose to buy one product or another. If the price of one item goes up, they can buy another instead—demand is elastic. The fewer available substitutes, the more inelastic demand will be.

Does the purchase use a large portion of income? If the amount of income used to make a purchase is large, demand is likely to be elastic. It tends to be inelastic if the amount of income is small.

The answers for a particular product may not always be all yes or all no. In those cases, a judgment must be made as to the level of demand elasticity.

Section Wrap-up

Answer these questions to check your understanding of the entire section.

1. Why is it important for businesses to know a product's demand elasticity?

_____

_____

_____

2. What are two methods that a business can use to determine the demand elasticity for their product?

_____

_____

_____

Expository Writing

Compare and contrast the elasticity of meals at a restaurant to the inelasticity of staple groceries. Use the three questions to explain why the demand curves for the items are not affected in the same way by changes in price.

_____

_____

_____

_____

_____

_____

_____

_____

_____

_____

_____

What Is Supply?

Big Idea

As you read pages 117–125 in your textbook, complete this graphic organizer by describing the causes for a change in supply.

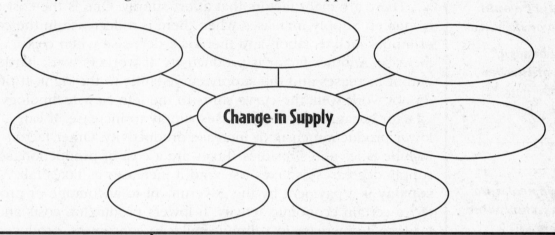

 **Notes** | **Read to Learn**

An Introduction to Supply *(page 118)*

Synthesizing Information

As you read, complete the sentence below:

A market supply curve is the sum of all _____ for one product in that market.

Supply is the amount of a product offered for sale at all possible market prices. According to the **Law of Supply,** suppliers will offer more products for sale at higher prices than they will offer at lower prices.

Similar to demand, supply can be shown in a table or graph. A **supply schedule** is a table that lists the various quantities of a product supplied at all possible prices. It shows that the **quantity supplied** rises when the price rises and that the quantity supplied falls when the price falls. The supply schedule data for a single producer in a market can be shown in a graph called the **supply curve.** Supply curves normally slope upward from the left to the right. As a result, price and quantity supplied have a direct relationship. The **market supply curve** is used to show the quantities offered by *all* producers that offer the same product for sale in a given market.

A **change in quantity supplied** is the change in amount offered for sale in response to a price change, or a movement along an individual or market supply curve. It is the interaction of both supply and demand that usually determines the final price of a product.

Notes | Read to Learn

Change in Supply (page 120)

Evaluating Information

For each of the situations below determine if the supply of the product would increase or decrease:

1. New houses if the cost of lumber increases:
Explain:

_____

_____

2. Cars if new automated assembly lines are invented:
Explain:

_____

_____

3. Pharmaceuticals if patents expire:
Explain:

_____

_____

Several causes can contribute to a **change in supply**—when suppliers offer different amounts of products for sale at all market prices. In this situation, the quantity changes even though the price does not. The data plotted on a supply curve appears as a shift to the right when supply increases, and a shift to the left when it decreases.

There are eight factors that affect supply. One is the cost of resources. Supply increases when there is a decrease in the cost of inputs such as labor, and there is a decrease when costs increase. Another factor is productivity. If workers work harder, output increases and the supply curve shifts to the right. If they do not work well, the curve shifts to the left. New technology is a factor because it usually causes supply to increase. It can lower production costs or increase productivity. Other factors include taxes and subsidies. Taxes are a cost of production, so supply decreases as taxes rise, and it increases as taxes fall. A **subsidy** is a payment by the government to encourage or protect a certain economic activity. It lowers production costs and leads to an increase in supply. Similar to consumers, producers have market expectations. If producers expect their product's prices will rise, they may make more causing the supply curve to shift right. If producers expect their product's prices to fall, they may produce something else or stop production. As a result, the curve will shift left. Government regulations add to production costs and cause a decrease in supply. Relaxed regulations, however, lead to an increase. The number of sellers is a factor that only relates to the market supply curve. If more firms enter the market, supply increases. If they leave, supply decreases.

Elasticity of Supply (page 124)

Comparing and Contrasting

What is the difference between demand elasticity and supply elasticity?

_____

_____

_____

Supply elasticity is a measure of how the quantity supplied responds to a change in price. Supply is *elastic* if a price increase leads to a proportionally larger increase in production; *inelastic* if a price increase leads to a proportionally smaller increase in production; and *unit elastic* if a price increase leads to a proportional change in production.

How a producer makes goods determines the elasticity of its supply curve. If a producer can quickly adjust to new prices, then supply is likely to be elastic. If it cannot, supply is likely to be inelastic. Unlike demand elasticity, the number of substitutes does not affect supply elasticity, and neither does the ability to delay purchases, nor the portion of consumers' income in relation to price.

Chapter 5, Section 1

Section Wrap-up

Answer these questions to check your understanding of the entire section.

1. How do producers in a market economy usually react to an increase in the price of their products?

_____

_____

_____

2. Which factors of change in supply affect both the individual supply curve and the market supply curve?

_____

_____

_____

Expository Writing

Suppose you manage a pizza store which of the following situation below would most greatly reduce your output. Write a cause and effect essay explaining how. A. Your workers all get sick at the same time. B. The government increases taxes on all prepared food. C. A competitor opens up a store one block away.

_____

_____

_____

_____

_____

_____

_____

_____

_____

_____

_____

The Theory of Production

Big Idea

As you read pages 127–130 in your textbook, complete this graphic organizer by filling in what occurs during the three stages of production.

Stage I	Stage II	Stage III

Read to Learn

The Production Function (page 128)

Drawing Conclusions

As you read, complete the sentence below:

In order to find the marginal product of one additional worker, subtract

_____

_____

from the total product of the current number of workers.

The **production function** shows how a change in the amount of a single variable input changes total output.

Economists focus on the **short run** when they study production. The short run is so brief that only the amount of the variable input (usually labor) can be changed. Then we know that a change in the varible input (number of workers) is the cause of any change in output in the short run. (Other changes take place in the **long run,** a period long enough for a firm to adjust the amounts of *all* productive resources.)

In the first column of the production schedule, we list the number of workers. In the second column, we list the **total product**—the total output produced by each number of workers. From these two values, we can measure and list the **marginal product** in the third column, which is the *extra* output or change in total product due to the increase of one more units of input. When you add up all the marginal products for a particular amount of variable input, the sum equals the total product for that input. Therefore, if the marginal products of the two workers are 7 and 13, the total product is 7 plus 13, or 20.

Stages of Production (page 129)

Identifying the Main Idea

Underline the main idea of the second paragraph.

Making Generalizations

As you read, complete the sentence below:

A firm can identify which stage of production it is in by looking at the _____ product column.

Determining Cause and Effect

In Stage III, which factor causes total output to decrease?

_____

_____

_____

Every firm faces the problem of deciding how many workers to hire in the short run. To help, a firm can identify the three **stages of production** in its production schedule.

During Stage I, the marginal product for each additional worker increases. As more workers are added, they cooperate to make better use of the available equipment and to improve methods of production. In the production schedule of a printed T-shirt factory, for example, the first worker has a marginal product of 7 T-shirts, so the total product is 7 T-shirts. Adding the second worker causes both workers to be more productive. In fact, the marginal product of the second worker is greater than the marginal product of the first worker. In our printed T-shirt factory, the total product of the first worker is 7 T-shirts while the total product of two workers is 20 T-shirts. The marginal product of the second worker is 13 T-shirts. The rate in which marginal output increases shows us that total product has more than doubled as a result of adding one worker. Total output will continue to rise at an increasing rate as long as the addition of each new worker contributes more units to total product than the previous worker. As a firm sees its total output increase in this way, it will keep hiring more workers.

At some point a firm reaches Stage II, characterized by decreasing marginal returns. In Stage II, the total production keeps growing, but it grows by smaller and smaller amounts During Stage II, each additional worker makes a diminishing (yet still positive) contribution to total output. This phase, where output increases at a lesser rate as more units of variable input are added, is an example of the principle of decreasing or **diminishing returns.** In the example of the T-shirt factory, suppose that the addition of a fifth worker has a marginal product of 28 T-shirts, and the addition of a sixth worker has a marginal product of 20 T-shirts. The addition of a sixth worker, then, marks the beginning of Stage II in the production schedule because the increase of the total product with six workers is less than the increase of the total product with five workers.

Eventually firms find themselves in Stage III, characterized by negative marginal returns. This happens when a firm hires too many workers. Workers get in each other's way and work less efficiently. As a result, the total output decreases. Suppose that in the production schedule, the total product of 10 workers is 148 T-shirts while the total product of 11 workers is 145 T-shirts. The addition of an eleventh worker has a marginal product of *minus* three T-shirts. At that point, the total product for 11 workers is actually less than the total product for 10 workers.

Section Wrap-up

Answer these questions to check your understanding of the entire section.

1. How does the production function help business owners make a profit?

_____

_____

_____

2. Within which stage of production should a firm operate? Explain.

_____

_____

_____

Expository Writing

Think of a task, such as washing a car or cooking a meal, which you have completed by yourself. Describe the task and the main steps you took to complete the task. Then consider how the marginal product would change if you had the help of one other person, two other people, and three other people.

_____

_____

_____

_____

_____

_____

_____

_____

_____

_____

_____

_____

Cost, Revenue, and Profit Maximization

Big Idea

As you read pages 132–137 in your textbook, complete this graphic organizer by explaining how total revenue differs from marginal revenue. Then provide an example of each.

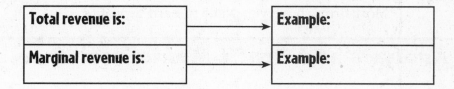

Total revenue is:	→	Example:
Marginal revenue is:	→	Example:

Notes | Read to Learn

Measures of Cost (page 133)

Evaluating Information

Write the following examples in the correct category below: lumber, salaries, computers (capital goods), transportation, and property taxes.

1. Fixed costs:

_____

_____

2. Variable costs:

_____

_____

Businesses use several measures of costs to make sure that they are operating efficiently.

Fixed costs, sometimes called **overhead,** remain the same regardless of the output of goods or services. Fixed costs include rent, insurance, and depreciation—the gradual wear and tear on capital goods through use over time.

Variable costs are production costs that change when the level of production changes. For example, labor costs change when workers work overtime or are laid off. Other examples include gasoline for delivery trucks and packaging supplies. The sum of all fixed costs and variable costs is the **total cost.**

Businesses find that **marginal cost** is the most useful measure of cost. It is the *extra* cost of producing one additional unit of output. For example, if the addition of one worker yields a marginal product of 7 units and increases variable costs by $90, each additional unit of output has a marginal cost of $12.86, or $90 divided by 7. In this way, the marginal cost per unit can be found for each additional worker. As a result, a firm knows the cost of producing each new unit of output as variable costs rise.

Applying Cost Principles (page 135)

Making Generalizations

Underline the facts in the passage that support the following statement. E-commerce booksellers have lower fixed costs than bookstores located in shopping centers.

Fixed and variable costs affect the way a business chooses to operate. For this reason, many stores are doing business on the Internet. Businesses engaged in **e-commerce**—an electronic business conducted over the Internet—reduce their fixed costs in many ways. They do not have to rent a building for their store(s) or hold inventory. For a fraction of a physical store's cost, a virtual store can show their products, make transactions, and reach more markets.

When a business knows its total costs, it can determine how many goods and services it must produce for its total costs to equal its total revenue. This is called the **break-even point.** Most firms, however, want to earn a profit.

Marginal Analysis and Profit Maximization (page 136)

Synthesizing Information

In which stage of production is the profit-maximizing quantity of input most likely to be reached? Explain:

_____

_____

_____

_____

_____

Businesses use two key measures to find the level of production that will generate the greatest profit—total revenue and marginal revenue. **Total revenue** is the total amount a firm earns. Put simply, total revenue is equal to the number of units sold multiplied by the average price per unit. For example, if 148 units of total output sell for $15 each, total revenue is $2,220. **Marginal revenue** is the more important measure. It is the extra revenue from the sale of one additional unit of output. Businesses find their marginal revenue by dividing the change in total revenue by the marginal product. Suppose, for example, a firm that has five workers, produces 90 units of output, and generates $1,350 of total revenue. Then they hire a sixth worker and output increases by 20 units so that the firm's total revenues increase to $1,650. Divide the total revenue change ($300) by the marginal product (20) and you get marginal revenue of $15. The marginal revenue earned by the sale of one more unit will always be $15, as long as every unit of output sells for $15. In the real world, however, marginal revenues often vary.

Marginal analysis is a way to make an informed decision by comparing the extra costs of doing something to the benefits gained from it. For businesses, this means gradually adding variable inputs (for example, workers) and then comparing the extra benefit (marginal revenue) to the extra cost (marginal cost). As long as marginal cost is less than marginal revenue, the business can continue to increase its variable inputs. Eventually, marginal cost and marginal revenue are equal, and the **profit-maximizing quantity of input** is reached. This means the firm has reached its greatest total profit. If marginal cost exceeds marginal revenue, profits will begin to fall.

Section Wrap-up

Answer these questions to check your understanding of the entire section.

1. Why is labor an important variable cost for most businesses?

_____

_____

_____

2. What happens when marginal cost of producing a product continues to be greater than marginal revenue of a product?

_____

_____

_____

Persuasive Writing

Write an essay that argues against government regulations, such as laws governing hiring, worker safety, and pollution controls. Support your argument by describing how government regulations affect costs, revenue, and profit maximization.

_____

_____

_____

_____

_____

_____

_____

_____

_____

_____

_____

Prices as Signals

Big Idea

As you read pages 143–146 in your textbook, complete this graphic organizer by explaining the advantages of prices.

 **Read to Learn**

Advantages of Prices (page 144)

Formulating Questions

Before you read about the advantages of prices, write two questions you think the passage will answer.

1. _____

_____

_____

2. _____

_____

_____

A **price** is the monetary value of a product as established by supply and demand. Prices act as signals that help people make economic decisions. Prices also give information that helps producers and consumers answer three basic questions of what, how, and for whom to produce. Prices perform the important task of helping the economy run smoothly. Prices perform their job effectively for several reasons.

First, prices are considered neutral—they favor neither the producer nor the consumer. Prices represent compromises or agreements between buyers and sellers. Secondly, prices in a market economy are flexible. The price system can absorb the effect of unexpected events on supply and demand, such as natural disasters. Buyers and sellers adjust their consumption and production behavior to meet changing needs and markets. Thirdly, people are familiar with prices and find prices easy to understand. Knowing the exact price of an item helps people make economic decisions quickly. Finally, prices do not add any administrative costs to products. In competitive markets, prices gradually adjust up or down without any one person making decisions or passing laws.

Allocations Without Prices (page 145)

Evaluating Information

Describe a set of criteria for allocating ration coupons. Then describe why two people might see the criteria as unfair.

_____

_____

_____

_____

_____

_____

_____

In countries with command economies, criteria other than prices are used to make economic decisions. **Rationing** is one example. It is a system in which a government decides consumers' "fair" share by issuing a ticket called a **ration coupon.** The coupon entitles the holder to obtain a certain amount of a product. It might be given to people outright, or the government might charge a fee that is less than the product's market value.

What problems does a rationing system cause? One problem is that many consumers come to believe that their share is too small. It is difficult to allocate rationing coupons in a way that everyone sees as fair.

Using rationing coupons results in heavy administrative costs—such as workers' salaries, printing, and distribution. Also, there is the possibility that coupons will be stolen, sold, or counterfeited to obtain a product intended for someone else.

A third problem that comes with rationing is its negative effect on the incentive to produce. When people receive the same number of coupons without the possibility of earning more, they lose their motivation to work harder. There is no economic reward for a greater effort.

Prices as a System (page 146)

Problems and Solutions

What problem do rebates solve?

_____

_____

_____

Economists favor the price system because nonprice allocation systems present so many problems. As previously discussed, prices help individuals within a specific market make decisions. Prices also serve as signals that help allocate resources between markets. This is because in times of high inflation, consumers spend their money on necessities, rather than non-essential items.

For example, if the price of electricity rises greatly, manufacturers of electric furnaces and boilers will notice a decrease in sales. As a result, the electric furnace manufacturers' inventories will grow too large. In such a case, the manufacturer may offer consumers a **rebate,** or a partial refund of the original price of the product.

Companies can also reduce their production of specific equipment. They may even have to close plants and reduce the number of their employees. These shifts of resources are natural and necessary in a market economy. In this way, prices allocate resources between markets. Prices are a system, or part of an informational network that links all markets in the economy.

Section Wrap-up

Answer these questions to check your understanding of the entire section.

1. How do prices help people make economic decisions?

_____

_____

_____

2. Explain the natural and necessary shifts of resources in a market economy.

_____

_____

_____

Descriptive Writing

Write a story that describes what it might be like to live in a country with a command economy that uses rationing to distribute goods. Include details such as where the characters of the story work and shop.

_____

_____

_____

_____

_____

_____

_____

_____

_____

_____

_____

_____

The Price System at Work

Big Idea

As you read pages 148–154 in your textbook, complete this graphic organizer by describing how a surplus and a shortage affect prices, demand, and supply.

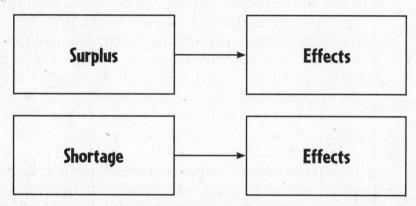

| Surplus | → | Effects |

| Shortage | → | Effects |

Notes   Read to Learn

The Price Adjustment Process *(page 149)*

Comparing and Contrasting

1. How are the goals of buyers and sellers different?

_____

_____

2. How are the motivations of buyers and sellers similar?

_____

_____

The process of establishing a price in a market economy is complicated because buyers and sellers have different goals, and transactions are voluntary. This requires compromise.

Economists use an economic model to illustrate the price adjustment process. One **economic model,** called a market demand and supply curve, allows us to analyze how the interaction of buyers and sellers results in a price that is agreeable to all market participants. In this graph, the supply and demand curves intersect at a specific point—**equilibrium price.** This is the price at which the number of units produced equals the number of units sold.

Surpluses and **shortages** are the market forces which push prices towards an equilibrium. A surplus occurs when the quantity supplied is greater than the quantity demanded at a given price. Prices drop as a result of the surplus. A shortage occurs when the quantity demanded is greater than the quantity supplied at a given price. Both price and the quantity supplied will then rise. The marketplace actually sets the prices, which allows both buyers and sellers to contribute to price adjustment.

Explaining and Predicting Prices *(page 152)*

Predicting

Would you expect to pay a high or low price for each of the goods below. Explain:

1. A ticket to a championship basketball game.

_____

_____

2. A Cher CD

_____

_____

3. An portable emergency generator right before a hurricane

_____

_____

4. A plain white T-shirt

_____

_____

5. The newest video game console

_____

_____

Looking at market models helps economists explain changes in prices. Changes in supply, changes in demand, or changes in both affect prices. Economists also consider elasticity when they predict how prices will change.

A change in supply, such as a shortage or a surplus, affects the price of a good or service. When supply is greater than expected, prices will be lower than predicted. And when supply is less than expected, prices will be higher than predicted.

A change in demand also affects the price of a good or service. Many factors affected the market demand for goods and services. These include changes in income, tastes, prices of related products, expectations, and the number of consumers. If the market model indicates a modest increase in demand from the expected demand, prices would increase. If the model indicates a decrease in demand from the expected demand, prices would decrease.

Simultaneous changes in both supply and demand also affects prices. As you know, an increase in demand would increase prices. But an unforeseeable event, such as a natural disaster, could cause supply to decrease at the same time and prices would increase even more. A combination of increased demand and decreased supply can lead to the highest possible prices.

Whenever supply or demand for a product fluctuates, the elasticity of the supply and demand curves affects how much prices change. When the change in price is relatively large for both supply and demand, the curves are inelastic. If one or both curves are elastic, the changes in price will be smaller. Therefore economists predict price changes more accurately by knowing the elasticity of each curve as well as the underlying factors affecting the supply and demand curves.

The price system is more efficient when markets are competitive because they allocate resources efficiently. Sellers lower the prices of their goods to compete and meet consumer demands. The competition among buyers for a limited supply of goods or services helps prevent prices from falling too low.

Section Wrap-up

Answer these questions to check your understanding of the entire section.

1. Explain how a market determines the equilibrium price.

_____

_____

_____

2. Why is it useful to predict changes in prices?

_____

_____

_____

Informative Writing

Price gouging is when sellers increase their prices above the market value. Describe a situation in which sellers would do so and in which buyers might be forced to pay higher prices.

_____

_____

_____

_____

_____

_____

_____

_____

_____

_____

_____

Chapter 6, Section 3 (Pages 156–161)

Social Goals and Market Efficiency

Big Idea

As you read pages 156–161 in your textbook, complete this graphic organizer by explaining the effects of price ceilings and price floors.

Policy	Effects
Price ceiling	
Price floor	

Notes

Read to Learn

Distorting Market Outcomes (page 157)

Synthesizing Information

How might price floors and price ceilings prevent buyers and sellers from receiving accurate information?

_____

_____

_____

_____

Federal, local, and state governments can regulate prices to achieve social goals. They can set a **price ceiling**—the highest legal price that can be charged for a product—when they think the equilibrium price is too high. Governments can set a **price floor**—the lowest legal price that can be paid for a good or service—when they think the equilibrium price is too low.

Rent control is one example of a price ceiling. A price ceiling, like any other price, affects how resources are divided and used. Rent control causes some productive resources, such as those used to build and maintain apartments, to slowly leave the rental housing market. Limiting the price charged for rent gives current renters an advantage, however, their apartments and buildings may fall into disrepair.

Minimum wage is one example of a price floor. Most economists argue that it increases the number of unemployed, because employers cannot afford to hire as many workers. Others argue that the minimum wage is unimportant because, in many areas, it is lower than the lowest wages paid. The minimum wage does, however, raise the income of the working poor.

 **Notes**

Read to Learn

Agricultural Price Supports *(page 159)*

Making Inferences

1. Why would agricultural prices be less stable than the prices of other goods and services?

_____

_____

_____

_____

2. Why does the government protect the economic stability of farmers more than other producers?

_____

_____

_____

_____

During the Great Depression, the price of agricultural goods was severely affected. The government tried to solve this problem by creating the Commodity Credit Corporation (CCC). The first solution employed by the CCC was to set **target prices,** or a price floor to stabilize farm prices. Later the CCC implemented a program that combined a **nonrecourse loan** with the target prices. This type of loan does not carry a penalty, and the borrower is not obliged to repay it. Farmers could choose to repay the loan in full with funds or if they failed to earn enough funds from sales, they could partially repay it with crops.

Although the CCC's loan program helped farmers, it created problems for the U.S. Department of Agriculture. It soon owned huge stockpiles of food. The CCC devised a new program based on a **deficiency payment** system—the government paid farmers the difference between the market price and the target price.

Both programs continued and became too expensive by the 1980s. Again, the government revised its approach. Experts suggested that it should try to discourage farming. This was the goal of the Conservation Reserve Program of 1985. It paid farmers to place their previously farmed land in a "land bank."

Two more recent programs tried to encourage farmers to respond to supply and demand. The government passed the Federal Agricultural Improvement and Reform Act (FAIR) in 1996. In 2002, Congress replaced FAIR with the Farm Security and Rural Investment Act. Unfortunately, the programs actually increased the total price support payments made by the government. As a result, American agriculture is more dependent on subsidies today than ever before.

When Markets Talk *(page 161)*

Predicting

As you read, complete the sentence below:

People and groups in an economy who listen to the market are able to _____

_____.

When people say that markets "talk" they mean that markets send us signals when prices move up or down in reaction to events that happen in other parts of the economy.

Suppose, for instance, that the price of oil greatly increased. If investors thought the increase in price was likely to continue, investors might sell stock as they anticipate smaller profits from corporations. An increase in oil prices would result in a decrease in disposable income for both investors and consumers, and corporations would incur higher operating costs. A significant drop in the stock market may tell the Federal Reserve Bank to lower interest rates. It may also tell investors to buy gold. In this example, the price of oil sent a signal to investors. Their actions sent a signal to the government and other investors.

Section Wrap-up

Answer these questions to check your understanding of the entire section.

1. What are two ways in which the government tries to work towards the goal of economic equity?

_____

_____

_____

2. How do agricultural price supports send inaccurate signals to farmers?

_____

_____

_____

Expository Writing

Suppose that your family has owned and worked a farm since the late 1800s. Think about whether or not you would like to farm the land as your family has done for generations. Write a diary entry analyzing your decision. Remember to include some of the farm subsidies that have helped keep the farm running over the years.

_____

_____

_____

_____

_____

_____

_____

_____

_____

_____

_____

Chapter 7, Section 1 (Pages 169–177)
Competition and Market Structures

Big Idea

As you read pages 169–177 in your textbook, complete this graphic organizer by identifying the characteristics of different market structures.

Market Structure	Characteristics
Perfect competition	

 **Notes** | **Read to Learn**

Perfect Competition (page 170)

Identifying the Main Idea

As you read about perfect competition, write down the main idea of the second paragraph in your own words.

_____

_____

_____

_____

_____

_____

_____

In the late 1700s, governments followed an economic philosophy known as **laissez-faire** (French for "allow them to do") and did not interfere much with businesses. Today, different conditions determine **market structure**—the nature and degree of competition among firms in the same industry. Economists classify market structures into four groups: perfect competition, monopolistic competition, oligopoly, and monopoly.

In a **perfect competition** market, the forces of supply and demand determine the equilibrium price. This means the firm that is the perfect competitor, or "price-taker," sets the price and determines the level of output that must reached to earn the greatest profit. A perfect competition market consists of a large number of buyers and sellers who exchange identical products; are able to act independently; are well-informed about the competition; and are free to enter into, conduct, or get out of business. Few markets meet all of these five conditions and yet perfect competition markets are ideal. Economists use to them to evaluate less competitive, or **imperfect competition** market structures, which have higher prices and fewer products.

Notes | Read to Learn

Monopolistic Competition *(page 173)*

Comparing and Contrasting

Underline the three main differences between perfect competition and monopolistic competition.

Monopolistic competition has all the conditions of perfect competition except that the products are not identical. Products in this type of market are generally similar. Competitors, however, try to win sales through **product differentiation** by calling attention to the real or perceived differences between their products and competing products in the same industry. To make consumers believe that one product is better than a competitor's, monopolistic competitors use **nonprice competition,** such as advertising, giveaways, or other promotions. A monopolistic competitor maximizes profit by charging a higher price if they successfully convince consumers their product is better and different than another.

Oligopoly *(page 174)*

Problems and Solutions

Describe one problem consumers encounter in an oligopoly market.

_____

_____

_____

In an **oligopoly,** a few very large sellers dominate an industry. This means sellers tend to act together or they risk losing customers. For example, if one seller changes its price, the others will follow to attract new customers. This interdependent behavior sometimes takes the form of **collusion,** or a formal agreement to behave in a cooperative manner. One form of collusion is **price-fixing**—when firms agree to charge the same or similar prices for a product. Collusion is against the law because it restricts trade. The prices of products within an oligopoly are usually higher than prices determined under perfect and monopolistic competitions.

Monopoly *(page 175)*

Synthesizing Information

Although the costs of production may be _____, prices are usually _____ in a monopoly because _____ _____.

A **monopoly** is a market structure with only one seller for a particular product. There are different types of monopolies: natural, geographic, technological, and governmental. In **natural monopolies,** the costs of production remains low because of **economies of scale**—the average cost of production falls as the firm grows larger. **Geographic monopolies** occur when there is only one seller in a certain geographic area. Firms with ownership or control of a manufacturing method, process, or other scientific advances are **technological monopolies. Government monopolies** include public transportation and lotteries in some areas. Monopolies compare marginal costs with marginal revenue to find the profit-maximizing quantity of output. Because monopolies do not face any competitors or equilibrium price, they can set a very high price.

Section Wrap-up   *Answer these questions to check your understanding of the entire section.*

1. Why are perfect competition markets both rare and ideal?

_____

_____

_____

2. Compare and contrast how businesses maximize profits and set prices within monopolistic competition and a monopoly.

_____

_____

_____

Expository Writing   *Write an essay identifying and describing the market structure of the video game console industry. Explain how the nature of the market structure affects how the industry sets prices and maximizes profits.*

_____

_____

_____

_____

_____

_____

_____

_____

_____

_____

_____

_____

Chapter 7, Section 2 (Pages 179–183)
Market Failures

Big Idea

As you read pages 179–183 in your textbook, complete this graphic organizer by listing the effects of competition.

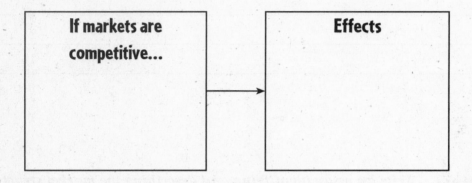

If markets are competitive...	→	Effects

Notes   Read to Learn

Types of Market Failures (page 180)

Formulating Questions

Before you read about types of market failures, write two questions that you think will be answered by the text.

1. _____

_____

2. _____

_____

Five conditions are necessary for competitive markets to exist. If a market does not meet all of these conditions, then a **market failure** occurs. One cause of market failure is inadequate competition. When larger and fewer firms dominate an industry, the decrease in competition allows firms to waste resources and collude.

Inadequate information about market conditions for buyers and sellers, such as wages, slows economic growth and can lead to market failure. Resource immobility is when land, capital, entrepreneurs, or labor cannot follow the highest prices. When a factory closes, many workers are unable to relocate.

Market failure also happens to **public goods.** They are products that everyone consumes, such as national parks and highways. The government funds public goods through taxation. However, the government does not always allocate the funds properly which can lead to a market failure.

Economic activities result in some kind of **externality**, or unintended side effect. Both **positive externalities** and **negative externalities** are market failures.

Read to Learn

Drawing Conclusions

Underline the facts that support the following conclusion.

If government did not make businesses stop overfishing, they would not stop on their own.

Analyzing Information

How is the vaccination market distorted?

_____

_____

Making Generalizations

As you read, complete the sentence below:

Externalities can result in the misdirection of the _____ or _____ of a particular business.

Externalities indicate a market failure because they distort or influence the economic decisions consumers and producers would normally make in a market. Ultimately, the influence of externalities results in a less efficient economy, and the government takes steps to correct the problem.

Overfishing is an example of negative externalities that distorts a market. One type of fish may become popular and as demand for that fish increases, the price rises. Then, more fishing boats harvest that type of fish from the ocean. The supply of that fish increases and the price drops accordingly.

In addition, the negative externality of overfishing causes several problems. First, fishing companies have an incentive to harvest that type of fish—there is a large market. Second, the resulting low market prices encourage more sales and lead to more fishing. Third, ocean ecosystems become unbalanced, and the species of fish can become extinct. Therefore, other people who depend on the ocean for their livelihood pay for the overfishing even if they do not buy the product.

The solution to the negative externalities of overfishing is for government to force the fishing companies to stop pursuing that fish by taxing or fining them. Companies then pass the cost of the taxes or fines to consumers by raising prices. Although higher prices might seem to be a problem, they actually help reverse the negative externality by decreasing demand. Also, the people who depend on the ocean ecosystem would not bear the cost of solving the problems caused by overfishing.

The distortion caused by positive externalities is evident in the vaccination market. Governments require their citizens to get vaccinated for infectious diseases mainly because through the success of vaccinations the threat of many diseases, such as smallpox, have been eliminated. From a purely economic perspective, a healthy population equals a more productive labor force and reduced medical costs.

Such positive externalities applied in the past when the U.S. government ordered millions of doses of the flu vaccine each year from only a few suppliers. The number of suppliers was limited because there was not enough incentive for additional businesses to produce the flu vaccine. In the recent past, there were serious shortages when one supplier's product became contaminated. Experts recommended that the government find ways to make the business of producing vaccines more profitable. Even though all businesses and individuals benefit from a healthy workforce, they do not pay the vaccine manufacturers in proportion to their benefit.

Section Wrap-up

Answer these questions to check your understanding of the entire section.

1. How can the government be responsible for market failure?

_____

_____

_____

2. How do externalities affect the prices in a market?

_____

_____

_____

Persuasive Writing

Think of a positive or negative externality that affects your community. Write a letter to a local legislator explaining how the externality distorts the economy and what steps should be taken by the government to correct it.

_____

_____

_____

_____

_____

_____

_____

_____

_____

_____

_____

_____

The Role of Government

Big Idea

As you read pages 185–189 in your textbook, complete this graphic organizer by describing how governments try to avoid market failures.

Government in Economic Affairs

Notes | Read to Learn

Maintain Competition (page 186)

Making Generalizations

Whose interests does antitrust legislation protect?

_____

_____

_____

_____

_____

Underline the facts in the passage that support your statement.

Fostering competitive markets is one of the best ways to protect scarce resources and satisfy consumers' needs. The government fosters competitive markets are by passing antitrust legislation and by setting regulations.

In the late 1800s, the United States began to pass laws to restrict monopolies and trusts. **Trusts** are illegal combinations of corporations or companies. Antitrust legislation prevents market failures by stopping companies from hindering competition. For example, Clayton Antitrust Act in 1914 outlawed **price discrimination**—the practice of selling the same product to different consumers at different prices. The Federal Trade Commission Act was passed that same year. It created the Federal Trade Commission (FTC) and gave it the authority to issue **cease and desist** orders that can require a company to stop an unfair business practice that reduces or limits competition.

It is not always best to break a monopoly up. Therefore, the government formed agencies to regulate various kinds of businesses. Companies involved in those businesses must argue their case for specific activities before a government agency. These agencies protect consumers' interests.

Improve Economic Efficiency (page 188)

Making Inferences

How would public disclosure requirements affect your decision to accept a lending company's credit card?

_____

_____

_____

_____

_____

_____

_____

The federal government has the ability to correct two market failures: inadequate information and public goods. Efficient and competitive markets depend on businesses making information about their products and their actions transparent to consumers. The requirement that business operate with some transparency is called **public disclosure.** Disclosure laws exist for companies that sell stock to the public. They also exist for companies that lend money to consumers. Lenders must explain how monthly interest is computed, the length of the loan, the amount of the payments, and other lending terms. Another example of public disclosure is "truth- in-advertising" laws which protect consumers by punishing sellers that make false claims about their products.

A free enterprise economy produces only a limited quantity of public goods. The government must provide things society values, such as education, museums, libraries, and highways. Many types of public goods increase the productivity of the economy. Some help to create an educated workforce that produces and purchases products. Others provide businesses with reliable and efficient transportation to move raw materials and final products.

Modified Free Enterprise (page 189)

Identifying the Main Idea

What is the main difference between the economy in the late 1800s and today's economy?

_____

_____

_____

_____

_____

_____

The United States economy has changed significantly over the past 200 years due to the government's increasing intervention. As a result the U.S. has a modified free enterprise economy. Today our economy is based on markets with varying degrees of government regulation.

In the late 1800s, many larger firms used their power to take advantage of smaller firms. Less competitive market structures, such as monopolies, led to a less efficient economy. The government stepped in by passing laws to protect workers and consumers.

In recent years, people have become more concerned with economic efficiency and the government's role in promoting it. Occasional interventions by the government keep markets reasonably competitive and the economy more efficient. People continue to debate the proper role of the government, but past economic activity has demonstrated that markets alone cannot meet all of consumers' wants and needs.

Section Wrap-up

Answer these questions to check your understanding of the entire section.

1. In what ways can the government foster competitive markets?

_____

_____

_____

2. Of what are the "truth-in-advertising" laws examples?

_____

_____

_____

Informative Writing

Write a speech presenting the benefits of a modified free enterprise economy to your economics class. Include facts about how this type of economy came into being, and detailed examples of how it benefits consumers.

_____

_____

_____

_____

_____

_____

_____

_____

_____

_____

_____

_____

_____

The Labor Movement

Big Idea

As you read pages 197–205 in your textbook, complete this graphic organizer by noting major events in the history of the U.S. labor movement on the time line.

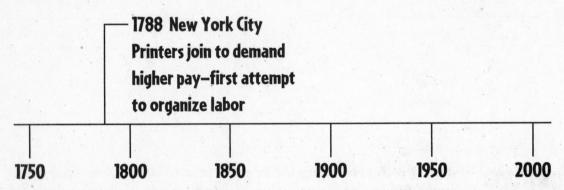

1788 New York City Printers join to demand higher pay–first attempt to organize labor

1750   1800   1850   1900   1950   2000

Notes   Read to Learn

Colonial Times to the 1930s *(page 198)*

Making Generalizations

How do strikes, picketing, and boycotts pressure employers to meet union demands?

_____

_____

_____

_____

_____

Organized labor first formed in 1778 when a group of printers demanded a raise. Unions were uncommon until after the American Civil War increased the prices of and the demand for goods and services. These factors spurred the growth of industrial jobs and the need to protect workers. In the post-Civil War period, there were **craft unions** or **trade unions** (workers skilled in a particular kind of work) and **industrial unions** (workers in the same industry).

Unions helped workers negotiate with their employers for higher pay, job security, and better hours and working conditions. Workers would **strike** in hopes of pressuring their employers to meet their demands. Other tactics included **picketing**—parading in front of an employer's business, and organizing **boycotts**—a mass refusal to buy a company's products.

Employers and the courts disliked union activity. Employers usually retaliated with **lockouts**, refusing to allow employees to work. Sometimes, management responded by setting up **company unions**. Other times struggles between unions and employers led to violence.

Labor Since the 1930s (page 201)

1. Why would the U.S. government oppose unions?

_____

_____

_____

_____

2. How might unions hinder economic efficiency?

_____

_____

_____

_____

Attitudes toward unions changed during the **Great Depression.** As it was the worst period of economic decline in American history, the Great Depression united factory workers by highlighting problems that they shared. In response, Congress passed a series of laws protecting workers that are still in effect today.

These new laws addressed unfair labor practices. The Norris-LaGuardia Act of 1932 was one such law that prevented courts from ruling against peaceful union activities. The Fair Labor Standards Act of 1938 prohibited children under 16 from working at all and children under 18 from doing work that endangered their health.

After World War II, partially due to the fear of Communists, public opinion shifted again against unions. Congress passed the Taft-Hartley Act of 1947. It allowed individual states to pass **right-to-work laws,** making it illegal to require workers to join unions. Congress passed additional laws such as the Labor-Management Reporting and Disclosure Act, or Landrum-Griffin Act of 1959. This law required unions to report their finances to the government and limited the amount of money union officials could borrow from unions.

In 1955 two of the largest unions, the American Federation of Labor and the Congress of Industrial Organizations (AFL-CIO), combined. Other important unions are **independent unions,** or unions that do not belong to the AFL-CIO, such as the Change to Win Coalition.

Organized Labor Today (page 203)

Predicting

Do you think union membership will increase or decrease in future decades? Explain.

_____

_____

_____

Unionized workers participate in four different kinds of union arrangements. In a **closed shop,** employers agree to only hire union members. However, the Taft-Hartley Act of 1947 banned all closed shop unions. In a **union shop,** workers must join a union after being hired. A **modified union shop** workers choose to join a union after being hired. Once they join, they must remain in the union for as long as they stay on the job. An **agency shop** also gives workers a choice, but it requires all workers, even nonunion workers, to pay union dues.

The United States **civilian labor force** is about 150 million people strong, which consists of individuals 16 years old or older who have a job or are looking for a job. Only about 12.5 percent of the American workers belong to a union. The size of union membership differs among demographic groups, states, and industries.

Section Wrap-up

Answer these questions to check your understanding of the entire section.

1. How is American History relevant to the study of the American economy?

_____

_____

_____

2. Which laws has Congress passed in favor of unions and fair working conditions and which laws has Congress passed against unions?

_____

_____

_____

Descriptive Writing

Write a diary entry of a coal miner in 1935 after attending a union meeting in which members discussed going on strike. Describe what his or her typical day is like at the coal mine and what working conditions need to be improved. Explain both the pros and cons of going on strike that union members would consider.

_____

_____

_____

_____

_____

_____

_____

_____

_____

_____

_____

Wages and Labor Disputes

Big Idea

As you read pages 207–213 in your textbook, complete this graphic organizer describing the different ways that labor disputes are resolved.

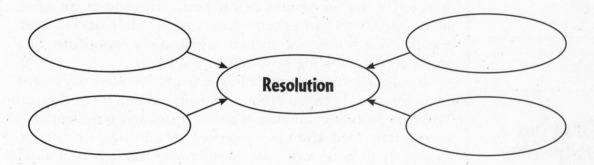

 **Notes** | **Read to Learn**

Wage Determination *(page 208)*

Synthesizing Information

What steps can you take to ensure that you receive a high wage during your career?

_____

_____

_____

_____

_____

Different levels of training and different occupations have a different **wage rate,** the standard amount paid to workers. In some cases, wage rates differ within the same occupation.

Differing wage rates occur for four reasons. First, there are four noncompeting categories of labor. Each category has a different skill and knowledge level: **unskilled labor, semiskilled labor, skilled labor,** and **professional labor.** People with jobs that require the most skills and training receive the highest wage. The **market theory of wage determination** states that supply and demand determine wage or salary. It also explains differing wage rates. In a market, supply and demand meet at the **equilibrium wage rate,** or the wage rate at which the labor market does not have a surplus or a shortage.

The **theory of negotiated wages** states that the bargaining strength of organized labor helps determine wages. Unions tend to offer higher wages for **seniority,** or the length of time a laborer holds a job. The fourth reason for differing wage rates is called the **signaling theory**—employers pay more to the people with certificates and degrees that indicate superior knowledge or ability.

Read to Learn

Resolving Labor Disputes (page 211)

Making Inferences

What factors motivate both unions and management to reach an agreement quickly?

_____

_____

_____

Drawing Conclusions

What might have happened if the government had not seized the bituminous coal industry in 1946?

_____

_____

_____

Analyzing Information

In which of the following industries might the government intervene to prevent a strike? Explain.
Nurses at a private hospital, guards at a private security company, or public school teachers.

_____

_____

Unions bargain with management over job-related matters. **Collective bargaining** is the process of negotiations between labor and management over issues such as pay, working hours, and health-care coverage. Elected union officials represent workers while company officials, who are in charge of labor relations, represent management. Successful negotiations require compromise from both sides. It is not surprising that negotiations might last for months before both parties reach an agreement. Once both parties settle their dispute, they draw a final contract, which may also include a **grievance procedure,** or a provision for resolving problems in the future.

If collective bargaining fails, there are five ways to resolve the differences between labor and management: mediation, arbitration, fact-finding, injunction and seizure, and presidential intervention. **Mediation** is the process of allowing a neutral third party to settle a dispute. Neither side has to accept a mediator's decision. The mediator might be one person or several people who recommend(s) a compromise on which both sides can agree. In **arbitration,** the third party's decision is final. Since both sides must agree to the final decision, this kind of negotiation is also called **binding arbitration.**

Sometimes unions and management settle disputes by **fact-finding,** which is an agreement for a neutral third party to collect facts about a dispute and present nonbinding recommendations. This process is especially useful when both sides have distorted the issues to gain public support, or when one side simply does not believe the other side's claims.

Another way to settle disputes is through seizure or **injunction,** a court order not to act. Unions can use injunction to direct a company not to lock out its workers. A **seizure** occurs when the government temporarily takes over operations while negotiating with a union. In 1946, for instance, the government seized the bituminous coal industry. Meanwhile, the government continued operating the mines as government officials worked out a settlement with the miners' union.

The final way to settle a labor-management dispute is by presidential intervention. First, the President of the United States may appeal to both parties to resolve their differences. Presidential intervention is not common, and this type of settlement works best if the appeal has broad public support. The president can also intervene by firing federal workers. Lastly, the president has emergency powers to end labor disputes. For example, in 1997, President Bill Clinton used a 1926 federal law, the Railway Labor Relations Act, to end an airline pilots' strike.

Section Wrap-up

Answer these questions to check your understanding of the entire section.

1. Explain what factors influence each theory: the market theory of wage determination and the theory of negotiated wages.

   _____

   _____

   _____

2. What is the difference between arbitration and mediation?

   _____

   _____

   _____

Persuasive Writing

Suppose you are a teacher who wants to motivate your students to work hard and go to college. You decide to write a persuasive letter intended for both the students and their parents. In your letter, discuss the four reasons that explain the differences in wage rate.

_____

_____

_____

_____

_____

_____

_____

_____

_____

_____

_____

Chapter 8, Section 3 (Pages 215–221)
Employment Trends and Issues

Big Idea

As you read pages 215–221 in your textbook, complete this graphic organizer to explain why women face an income gap.

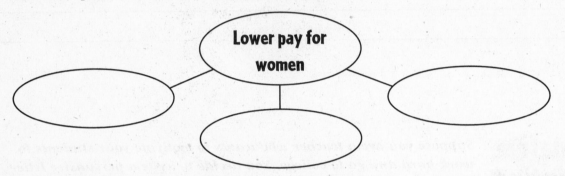

Lower pay for women

Notes   ## Read to Learn

Decline of Union Influence (page 216)

Synthesizing Information

How have the market forces of supply and demand affected the influence of unions?

_____

_____

_____

_____

_____

A downward trend in both membership and influence of labor unions is evident in today's economy. Since union wages tend to be higher than nonunion wages, union products cost more. In a competitive market, the demand for union-made products will be lower than nonunion- or foreign-made products.

Recently employers have sought to scale back unions or keep unions out of their business all together. By asking for givebacks or establishing a two-tier wage system employers have scaled back union wages. A **giveback** is a wage, fringe benefit, or work rule that the union gives up. A **two-tier wage system** pays new workers a lower wage than existing workers. Employers also deter unions when they include workers in their management team. A few have even filed bankruptcy to void union contracts.

Workers are also responsible for the declining influence and membership of unions. Today, more Americans work a second job to make ends meet, and they do not have the time to form or even to support a union. Also, today's workforce includes more women and teenagers, who are often less loyal to unions.

 **Notes** | **Read to Learn**

Lower Pay for Women (page 217)

Evaluating Information

Have the U.S. government's attempts to remedy discrimination been successful?

_____

_____

_____

_____

Women earn substantially less than men in the workforce. Economists identify three reasons for the gender-income gap. The main reason is discrimination in the labor market. Women and minorities often reach a **glass ceiling.** This invisible barrier stops them from further promotion. The second reason for the income gap is the uneven distribution of men and women among occupations. For example, men tend to dominate construction jobs, while women dominate office jobs. Finally the income gap is also a result of the difference in education and experience of men compared to women. Working women have lower education levels than men and are likely to drop out of the workforce to raise families, limiting their experience.

The government has legal remedies to counter wage and salary discriminations. The Equal Pay Act of 1963 prohibits wage and salary discrimination for jobs requiring equivalent skills and responsibilities for men and women on the same jobs in the same businesses. Another law, the Civil Rights Act of 1964, prohibits discrimination based on gender, race, color, religion, and national origin. Market remedies such as using **set-aside contracts** also help overcome unfair hiring practices by reserving a contract or part of it for a minority group.

The Minimum Wage (page 219)

Detecting Bias

How can the same data about the minimum wage be shown to support opposing points of view?

_____

_____

_____

Minimum wage is the lowest wage employers can legally pay workers. Supporters argue that it furthers the economic goals of equity and security. Opponents, however, argue that minimum wage is counter to the goal of economic freedom.

There are three ways to express data to analyze trends in the minimum wage: current dollars, real or constant dollars, and percentage of average manufacturing wage. **Current dollars** shows minimum wage prices adjusted for inflation, which gives a distorted view. Although it shows that minimum wage has increased, inflation should not be removed from the analysis. Inflation affects workers' purchasing power.

Real dollars or **constant dollars** are prices adjusted for inflation. Computing real dollars requires using a **base year** that serves as a comparison for all other years. Real dollars show that if the minimum wage stays the same and inflation continues, then its purchasing power will continue to decline.

Economists sometimes express the minimum wage as a percent of the average manufacturing wage. From this analysis, economists predict a decline in minimum wage relative to the increase in the average manufacturing wage.

Chapter 8, Section 3

Answer these questions to check your understanding of the entire section.

1. How are both workers and employers responsible for the decline of unions?

_____

_____

_____

2. Why is it difficult to compare the minimum wage of today with the minimum wage of the past?

_____

_____

_____

Expository Writing

Suppose you are a reporter for your local newspaper. Your assignment is to write an article about how the gender income gap has affected one woman whom you know. Describe in detail her occupation, skills and experience, and the discrimination she has encountered. You can make up any details necessary to write your article.

_____

_____

_____

_____

_____

_____

_____

_____

_____

_____

_____

The Economics of Taxation

Big Idea

As you read pages 229–236 in your textbook, complete this graphic organizer by filling in the criteria for taxes to be effective. Then define each of the criteria in your own words.

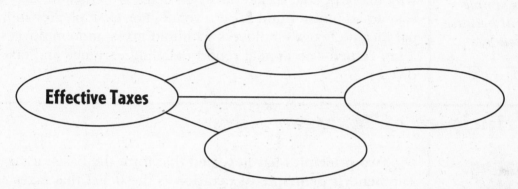

 **Notes** | **Read to Learn**

Economic Impact of Taxes *(page 230)*

Comparing and Contrasting

Would a sin tax imposed by a state be as effective as a federally imposed sin tax? Explain.

_____

_____

_____

_____

Taxes affect people's productivity, how resources are allocated, and how people behave. When the government imposes a tax, it raises the cost of production. Higher production costs result in higher prices. If higher prices lower demand, some firms cut production. Resources then shift to other industries.

The purpose of some taxes is to influence people's behavior. For example, the interest on a mortgage is tax deductible, which encourages homeownership. The purpose of a **sin tax** on cigarettes—a high tax which raises revenue and discourages the purchase of a product—is to discourage smoking.

Taxes can change productivity and growth by creating or reducing incentives. For example, some people argue that people will not strive to earn more if it means paying more taxes.

The final burden of a tax is called the **incidence of tax.** For example, a tax on a gas utility might be paid by the company or paid by the consumer in the form of higher prices. If demand is *elastic,* the producer is more likely to keep prices low to keep the level of demand the same. If demand is *inelastic,* the producer will more likely raise its prices.

Criteria for Effective Taxes *(page 232)*

Synthesizing Information

As you read, complete the sentence below:

Sales tax is simple and efficient because it is collected by _____.

In order to be effective, taxes must be equitable, simple, and efficient. Equitable means fair and just. Some tax laws have unfair **tax loopholes**—oversights that allow some people to avoid paying them. Tax laws should be simple. **Sales tax** is an example of a simple tax. It is added to the price of a product at the time of sale. Conversely, the **individual income tax**—the federal tax on people's earnings—is a complex tax, which is why many people dislike it. When taxes are efficient, they are easy to administer and raise revenue. For example, for individual income taxes, employers withhold taxes and employees file a **tax return**—an annual report detailing earnings and taxes owed.

Two Principles of Taxation *(page 234)*

Evaluating Information

Which principle of taxation best applies to the following: A city builds a marina for boat owners and needs to raise revenue to maintain it.

_____

Two principles have evolved that form the basis of taxes. The **benefit principle of taxation** is the belief that taxes should be paid according to the benefits received, regardless of income. Two limitations of this principle are that those who receive government services may be least able to pay for them and the benefits received are difficult to measure. The **ability-to-pay principle of taxation** is the belief that taxes should be paid according to the level of income, regardless of the benefits received. It is based on two factors. First, benefits received cannot always be measured. Secondly, people assume that those with higher incomes suffer less from paying taxes.

Three Types of Taxes *(page 235)*

Drawing Conclusions

As you read, complete the sentence below:

A progressive tax is based on the

_____

principle.

There are three types of taxes. The first, a **proportional tax,** imposes the same percentage rate of taxation, regardless of income. Thus the **average tax rate**—total tax paid divided by total taxable income—is constant. An example is the 1.45 percent tax that funds **Medicare**. Another type is a **progressive tax,** which imposes a higher percentage rate of taxation as income rises. It uses a progressively higher **marginal tax rate**—the tax rate that applies to the next dollar of taxable income. One example is the individual income tax. The third type is the **regressive tax,** which imposes a *lower* percentage rate of taxation as income rises. Sales tax is one example of a regressive tax because it amounts to a greater percentage of the earnings of low-income taxpayers than high-income taxpayers.

Section Wrap-up

Answer these questions to check your understanding of the entire section.

1. How do elastic demand and inelastic demand affect the incidence of a tax?

_____

_____

_____

2. Is a progressive tax an effective way to tax? Is it equitable, simple, and efficient?

_____

_____

_____

Persuasive Writing

Suppose you live in a city with declining services and high unemployment. Write a newspaper editorial that argues for or against a sales tax on food. Consider the economic impact of taxes and the effectiveness of taxes in your argument.

_____

_____

_____

_____

_____

_____

_____

_____

_____

_____

Federal, State, and Local Revenue Systems

Big Idea

As you read pages 238–245 in your textbook, complete this graphic organizer by identifying and describing three revenue sources each for federal, state, and local governments.

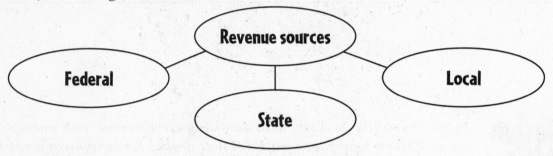

Revenue sources

Federal

Local

State

Notes | Read to Learn

Federal Government Revenue Sources *(page 239)*

Making Inferences

As you read, underline the sentence that supports the following inference.

Like individuals, the federal government must borrow money when it spends more funds than it receives.

The federal government receives revenue from three main sources. It collects individual income tax, its main revenue source, through a **payroll withholding system.** In this system, employers deduct income taxes from workers' paychecks and send that money to the **Internal Revenue Service (IRS).** Since taxpayers' income can increase because of inflation, the IRS offsets inflation by **indexing** or adjusting the income-tax brackets. Another source of revenue is **FICA,** the Federal Insurance Contributions Act tax, which pays for Social Security and Medicare. Both individual income tax and FICA are called **payroll taxes** because employers deduct it from paychecks. Borrowing by selling bonds is the third main source of revenue.

The fourth-largest source of all revenue is **corporate income tax.** Corporations pay a tax on their profits. An **excise tax** is a tax collected through the manufacture or sale of selected items. The **estate tax** collects revenue from the transfer of property of a deceased person while **gift taxes** collect revenue from the transfer of money. A **customs duty**—a tax on imported products—and miscellaneous fees are other sources of revenue.

 **Notes** | **Read to Learn**

State Government Revenue Sources *(page 242)*

Determining Cause and Effect

How might state revenue be affected by federal tax cuts?

_____

_____

_____

State governments collect their revenues from several sources, the largest being **intergovernmental revenue,** or from funds one level of government receives from another level of government. States receive these funds from the federal government to help pay for states' welfare, education, highway, health, and hospital expenses. **Sales tax**—a general state or city tax levied on a product at the time of sale—is the second-largest revenue source for most states. Merchants collect the taxes and pay the states periodically. Forty-five states have a general sales tax. Additionally, forty-three collect individual income tax. Keep in mind that both tax bracket divisions and types of taxes differ considerably from state to state.

Smaller sources of state government revenue include interest on surplus funds, higher education fees from state-owned educational institutions, corporate income taxes, and hospital fees.

Local Government Revenue Sources *(page 243)*

Evaluating Information

Why would raising property taxes be an effective way to increase a local government's revenue?

_____

_____

_____

_____

Local governments' two main sources of revenue consist of intergovernmental funds and property taxes. The largest portion of intergovernmental funds comes from the state to pay for education and public well-being. In addition, a much smaller portion of intergovernmental revenues comes directly from the federal government. **Property tax** on tangible and intangible possessions such as real estate, stocks, and bonds is another important source of revenue. Most of the revenue from property taxes comes from real estate. **Tax assessors** assign value and evaluate the value of property periodically so it is fairly taxed.

The third-largest source of income is from payments to public utilities. Many of these utilities are **natural monopolies**—a market structure in which the average cost of production is lowest when a single firm exists. In addition, many cities have their own sales taxes that are usually much less than state sales taxes. City sales tax is the fourth-largest source of local government revenues.

Local governments also generate income through hospital fees, income taxes, interest on invested funds, and borrowing funds. Overall, available revenue sources for local governments are very limited compared to state and local governments.

Section Wrap-up

Answer these questions to check your understanding of the entire section.

1. What federal programs does FICA support?

_____

_____

_____

2. Which sources of revenue for the federal government are not direct sources of revenue for state and local governments?

_____

_____

_____

Informative Writing

Suppose you are the mayor of Luckytown, which was recently very unlucky and lost 800 jobs due to plant closings. In order to solve the unemployment problem, the city and state council has passed a series of tax incentives to attract businesses to move there. Write a promotional letter describing these tax incentives to prospective businesses.

_____

_____

_____

_____

_____

_____

_____

_____

_____

_____

_____

_____

Current Tax Issues and Reforms

Big Idea

As you read pages 247–253 in your textbook, complete this graphic organizer by filling in the advantages and the disadvantages of the flat tax and the value-added tax. Include definitions of both taxes in your own words below the organizer.

	Advantages	Disadvantages
Flat tax		
Value-added tax		

 **Notes** | **Read to Learn**

Examining Your Paycheck (page 248)

Problems and Solutions

Why must workers file federal and state tax returns even though these taxes are already deducted from their paychecks?

_____

_____

_____

_____

_____

Employers usually deduct federal, state, and local taxes directly from workers' paychecks and list these withheld taxes on the **payroll withholding statement.** This stub summarizes pay, tax withholdings, and other deductions, and it is attached to the paycheck.

The amounts deducted for federal and state taxes are only estimates of how much workers owe, so individuals must settle any differences by filing federal and state tax returns between January 1 and April 15 of the next year. Since local taxes are usually small, most localities do not require taxpayers to file a separate tax return.

A payroll withholding statement also lists FICA taxes and voluntary deductions. Voluntary deductions may include contributions to retirement savings plans, money deposited in a credit union, union dues, health insurance payments, and disability insurance payments.

By reviewing his or her payroll withholding statement, a worker can calculate the percentage of earnings that he or she actually takes home for each pay period.

Tax Reform (page 249)

Analyzing Information

As you read, begin with the year 1981 and list the major tax reforms that took place, along with a brief explanation of the reform.

1. _____

2. _____

3. _____

4. _____

5. _____

6. _____

After years of tax reforms which raised or lowered taxes, the relationship between taxes and economic growth is still unclear. In 1981, the Economic Recovery Tax Act was passed to stimulate economic growth by reducing taxes for businesses and individuals. Businesses benefited from two aspects of the bill: **accelerated depreciation**—a schedule that spreads depreciation over fewer years—and **investment tax credit**—credit given for buying equipment.

Congress passed tax reform laws in 1986 to keep the rich from avoiding taxes altogether. This strengthened the **alternative minimum tax,** the personal income tax rate that applies when taxes fall below a certain level. Yet after 10 years of tax cuts, the federal government had to borrow more. In 1993, tax reform was passed so that the government could more easily balance the budget. At that time two more top marginal tax brackets were added. When the Republicans controlled Congress in 1994, they passed the Taxpayer Relief Act of 1997. It decreased the tax on inheritance and **capital gains,** or profits from selling assets held for at least one year. This law seemed to favor the wealthy and made the tax law more complex than ever before.

George W. Bush used the 2001 budget surplus to fund a tax reform that reduced the top four marginal tax brackets, introduced a 10 percent tax bracket, and eliminated the estate tax on the wealthiest 2 percent of taxpayers by 2010.

Alternative Tax Approaches (page 251)

Making Inferences

Why is the VAT tax controversial when it seems equitable, simple, and efficient?

_____

_____

_____

_____

One alternative to the personal income tax is a **flat tax,** a proportional tax on individual income after reaching a specified level. The advantages of a flat tax are that it is easy to calculate, it closes most tax loopholes, and it reduces the need for tax experts. Its disadvantages are that it removes the incentives for desirable behavior, it is unclear if it would spur economic growth, and it is difficult to find the right rate to replace current revenues.

Another alternative is the controversial **value-added tax (VAT),** a tax on the value added at every stage of the production process. The VAT is advantageous because it is hard to avoid, distributes tax evenly, is easy to collect, and may encourage people to save. The main disadvantage, however, is that the tax is virtually invisible. People would notice an increase in the price of final products, but would not know how much of the increase was due to taxes.

Section Wrap-up

Answer these questions to check your understanding of the entire section.

1. What are some of the reasons that the federal government has passed tax reform bills in recent years?

_____

_____

_____

2. How does the flat tax remove incentives for desirable behavior?

_____

_____

_____

Persuasive Writing

How do you feel about taxes and tax reform? After learning about federal, state, and local taxes, tax principals, and approaches to income taxes, what kind of tax reform do you think the country needs? Write a persuasive essay that states and supports your opinion on taxes.

_____

_____

_____

_____

_____

_____

_____

_____

_____

_____

_____

The Economics of Government Spending

Big Idea

As you read pages 261–265 in your textbook, complete this graphic organizer by listing reasons for the increase in government spending since the 1940s.

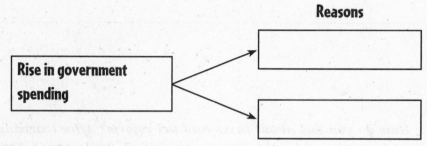

Reasons

Rise in government spending

Notes

Read to Learn

Government Spending in Perspective *(page 262)*

Evaluating Information

Label each expenditure below as pork or grant-in-aid:

1. A $100,000 for a boxing club in Nevada_____

2. A million dollar payment to a local government to repair a bridge_____

The use of **pork** in the federal budget has increased as **public-sector** spending has grown. Pork is a line-item budget expenditure that avoids normal budget procedures and benefits a small number of people or businesses. The public sector of the economy includes local, state, and federal governments while the **private sector** includes private individuals and businesses. Public-sector spending has increased since the 1930s for two reasons. First, people became more comfortable with it during the Great Depression, when the government created projects to stimulate the economy. In the 1940s, government spending during World War II created additional jobs, further increasing citizens' acceptance of the government's role in the economy.

The first type of government expenditure is in the form of goods and services, such as land, capital goods, and wages. The second type of expenditure is a **transfer payment,** or payment for which the government receives neither goods nor services in return. **Grants-in-aid** are special types of transfer payments from one level of government to another, such as aid to disaster stricken areas.

Notes | Read to Learn

Impact of Government Spending *(page 264)*

Making Inferences

Why does the government subsidize public transportation in big cities?

_____

_____

Analyzing Information

Describe a situation where a government decision indirectly affects the distribution of income.

_____

_____

Making Generalizations

As you read, complete the sentence below.

Businesses should be aware of government _____ and _____ which may affect their industry.

Because the public sector is such a large portion of the economy, federal, state, and even local spending affects people's lives in many ways, including resource allocation, the distribution of income, production in the private sector, and people's tax burden.

Government spending decisions affect the allocation of resources. For example, **subsidies** are a type of public sector spending that encourage or protect certain economic activities. Agriculture is one industry which receives various forms of subsidies. If agricultural subsidies were withdrawn, fewer factors of production would be used to produce agricultural products. These factors of production could then be used in other industries.

Regulatory decisions can also affect the economy. Simple decisions can start a chain reaction which alters the supply and demand of goods in a market. When the United States Food and Drug Administration (FDA) required that the nutrition labels on prepared foods include the amount of trans fatty acid, or trans fat, in foods, many prepared food producers, responded by reducing or discontinuing their use of ingredients with trans fat. As a result producers of vegetable oil, for example, responded by producing more oils with very low amounts or no trans fat and producing less oils with high amounts of trans fat.

Government spending also influences the **distribution of income,** or the way in which the nation's income is divided among families, individuals, or other groups. Increasing or decreasing transfer payments, such as Social Security and welfare, directly affect the incomes of people who receive financial support from the government. In addition, government decisions about what products and services to buy and from whom to buy them indirectly affects the distribution of income.

Sometimes public-sector goods and services compete with goods and services produced in the private sector. For example, private sector firms like United Parcel Service compete with the United States Postal Service, which is publicly subsidized, to provide parcel delivery service.

Tax revenues from both individuals and businesses support public-sector spending. Although people and businesses would prefer to pay less taxes, the trade off would be a decrease in government services.

Section Wrap-up

Answer these questions to check your understanding of the entire section.

1. Describe two ways that government spending affects income.

_____

_____

_____

2. Describe two ways in which government spending affects how resources are allocated.

_____

_____

_____

Persuasive Writing

Suppose you are a candidate for senator of your state. It is a very close election and the Army announces that it is going to close an important military base. The closing will result in the loss of 5,000 jobs. Write a campaign speech that addresses what you would do to solve the problem if elected.

_____

_____

_____

_____

_____

_____

_____

_____

_____

_____

_____

_____

Federal, State, and Local Government Expenditures

Big Idea

As you read pages 267–275 in your textbook, complete this graphic organizer by describing the different types of government spending.

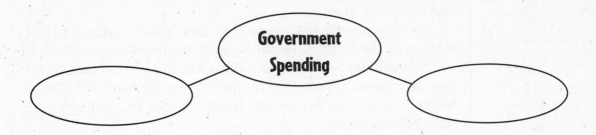

 **Notes** | **Read to Learn**

Federal Government Expenditures (page 268)

Determining Cause and Effect

How would a budget deficit affect mandatory spending?

_____

_____

_____

_____

_____

The **federal budget** is the annual plan outlining proposed spending and expected revenues for a **fiscal year,** the 12-month financial planning period. The budget process begins when the Office of Management and Budget (OMB) prepares a budget request. The House of Representatives assigns different components of the budget to 13 subcommittees. Each subcommittee prepares an **appropriations bill,** or piece of legislation authorizing spending for certain purposes. After the House and Senate approve the same version of the bill, it is sent to the president to sign. If projected expenditures in the federal budget are greater than projected revenues, there is a **budget deficit.** If revenues are greater than expenditures, there is a **budget surplus.**

Mandatory spending is federal spending authorized by law that continues without the need for annual approvals by Congress. Interest on debt, **Medicare,** a senior citizen health-care program, and **Medicaid,** a federal-state medical insurance program, are examples of mandatory expenditures.

Discretionary spending is spending that must be approved by Congress in the annual budgetary process.

State Government Expenditures (page 271)

(page 271)

Evaluating Information

Why don't state governments pay for Social Security and other income security programs?

_____

_____

_____

_____

Individual states also have to create and approve budgets. The budget approval processes varies among states. Some states have a **balanced budget amendment,** requiring the state government to spend no more than it collects in taxes and other revenues.

The largest category of state spending is **intergovernmental expenditures**—funds that one level of government transfers to another level for spending. These funds from sales taxes and other state revenue sources are distributed to local communities to pay for services, such as elementary and secondary education and fire protection.

Some expenditures are paid to individuals and are a large portion of the budget. Public welfare payments for medical care and to maintain welfare institutions are the second-largest category of expenditures. Contributions to retirement and insurance funds for state employees are another major expenditure of state governments.

A relatively small portion of a state's budget includes corrections facilities, utilities, hospitals, and parks in contrast to subsidies paid to state colleges and universities which are the fifth-largest state expenditure.

Local Government Expenditures (page 274)

Synthesizing Information

List two sources of revenue for local governments:

1. _____

2. _____

In local governments, an elected representative or group, such as the mayor or the city council, decide on a local budget. Specific budget processes vary from one local government to the next.

The expenses included in providing elementary and secondary education are usually the largest item in a local budget. These expenses consist of wages for teachers and staff, the cost of textbooks and supplies, and the cost of building and maintaining school buildings.

Local government spending includes paying for many services that people depend upon. The costs of providing public utilities, such as sanitation, natural gas, electricity, and water are in fact the second-largest portion of most local budgets. Expenditures associated with public safety and health are another large portion of local government budgets. Examples include the costs of having a fire department and police force. The remaining spending usually pays for highways, roads, and street repairs that are not covered by state budget.

Section Wrap-up

Answer these questions to check your understanding of the entire section.

1. Which body of the federal government has the most power over the budget: the House of Representatives, the Senate, or the Executive Office of the President?

   _____

   _____

   _____

2. How is the budget preparation process similar and different among federal, state, and local governments?

   _____

   _____

   _____

Expository Writing

Write a cause and effect essay that describes how a major snowstorm, hurricane, or flood in your area would affect the state and local governments' budgets for that year.

_____

_____

_____

_____

_____

_____

_____

_____

_____

_____

_____

Deficity, Surpluses, and the National Debts

Big Idea

As you read pages 277–283 in your textbook, list three attempts by government to reduce the federal deficit and the national debt, then explain the results of each attempt.

Attempt	Result

Notes

Read to Learn

From Deficits to Debt (page 278)

Making Inferences

When there is a balanced budget one fiscal year, does the national debt change? Explain:

_____

_____

_____

Annual government spending that exceeds government income from taxes and other revenues is called **deficit spending**. It is difficult to predict if or how much deficit spending will occur in a fiscal year.

When annual spending exceeds revenue, the federal government borrows funds, including selling securities to investors. Deficit spending over decades results in a substantial **national debt**—the total amount borrowed to finance deficit spending. The national debt can be expressed as a percentage of GDP or as a dollar amount **per capita**. A large portion of the national debt is borrowed from government **trust funds.** A trust fund is a special account used to hold revenues for a specific expenditure, such as Social Security. A **balanced budget** occurs when expenditures equal revenues.

Public debt owed by the government is different from private debt. Most importantly, the government cannot go bankrupt. The government owes most of the national debt to itself and does not have to repay its debt by a specific date. The government also does not give up purchasing power to repay debt.

Impact of the National Debt (page 280)

Determining Cause and Effect

List two ways that public debt affects individuals' incomes.

1. _____

2. _____

The national debt affects the economy by transferring purchasing power, reducing economic incentives, causing a crowding-out effect, and redistributing income. When public debt increases, taxes increase, transferring purchasing power from the private sector to the public sector. In addition, purchasing power is transferred from one generation of consumers to the next if debt incurred today is paid by future taxpayers. The national debt also affects the economy by reducing individuals' economic incentive to buy the goods and services they need instead of using government funds to pay for them. A third way that the national debt affects the economy is by increasing interest rates. When the government borrows a lot of funds, the higher-than-normal interest rates and diminished access to financial capital causes the **crowding-out effect.** In addition, national debt impacts the tax structure, which affects the distribution of income.

Reducing Deficits and the Debt (page 282)

Synthesizing Information

Are entitlements mandatory or an example of discretionary spending?

_____

_____

Congress has tried to reduce the national debt by passing legislation to change the budget process. Since the 1980s Congress has passed a range of legislation initiatives intended to balance the budget. In 1983, Congress ambitiously tried to mandate a balanced budget which failed as a result of a weak national economy. In 1990 Congress passed the Budget Enforcement Act, which contained a **"pay-as-you-go"** provision requiring new spending proposals or tax cuts to be offset by reductions in other areas of spending. In 1996 Congress gave the president a **line-item veto,** or the power to cancel specific budget items without rejecting the entire budget. The Supreme Court, however, ruled that this veto power was unconstitutional. In 1997, the government passed the Balanced Budget Agreement which placed **spending caps,** or limits on annual discretionary spending.

The deficit can also be controlled by increasing taxes and reducing spending. In 1993, President Clinton led Congress to pass legislation that increased taxes for the wealthiest taxpayers and reduced spending. This law, along with help from a strong economy, resulted in four years of budget surplus. Reducing federal spending is difficult because unplanned events require funds. **Entitlements**—programs using established eligibility requirements to provide health, nutritional, or income supplements—make up a large portion of the budget and are also very hard to reduce.

Section Wrap-up

Answer these questions to check your understanding of the entire section.

1. What is the relationship between public debt and the annual deficit or surplus?

_____

_____

_____

2. Explain the purpose of the presidential line-item-veto? Why did the Supreme Court rule that it was unconstitutional?

_____

_____

_____

Expository Writing

Write a compare and contrast essay from the perspective of a member of Congress about whether it is easier to raise revenues or decrease expenditures in order to balance the budget. Use historical examples from this section to support your conclusion.

_____

_____

_____

_____

_____

_____

_____

_____

_____

_____

_____

_____

Savings and the Financial System

Big Idea

As you read pages 289–294 in your textbook, complete this graphic organizer by describing how financial intermediaries channel money.

Financial intermediary	Way to channel money

 **Notes**   **Read to Learn**

Saving and Economic Growth (page 290)

Analyzing Information

Is any one part of a financial system more important than the others? Explain.

_____

_____

_____

_____

_____

Growth in an economic system depends on people **saving** funds. Note that the term *saving* means the absence of spending, while the term **savings** refers to the funds that become available for investors to borrow when other people save. There are many ways people can save. One way is to purchase a **certificate of deposit,** or a document showing that an investor has made an interest-bearing loan to a bank. Documents such as savings accounts, bonds, and certificates of deposit are **financial assets.** Financial assets are in fact claims on the income and property of the borrower and explain the amount and terms of the loan.

Savers and borrows interact in a financial system. A **financial system** is a network of savers, investors, and financial institutions that work together to transfer revenue to investors in a circular flow. The financial institutions in the network are called **financial intermediaries.** They lend the funds that savers provide.

Any sector of the economy can borrow and supply savings. Governments and businesses are the largest borrowers. Households and businesses provide the most savings.

Notes | Read to Learn

Nonbank Financial Intermediaries (page 292)

Making Inferences

What is the incentive for nonbank financial institutions to lend funds?

_____

_____

_____

_____

_____

_____

_____

Banks, credit unions, and savings associations transfer money from savers to borrowers. They obtain funds when they accept regular deposits. **Nonbank financial institutions** are nondepository institutions that also channel savings to borrowers. Examples of nonbank financial institutions are finance companies, life insurance companies, and pension funds. **Finance companies** specialize in making loans directly to consumers and buy installment loan contracts from merchants. They check a consumer's credit rating and make a loan only if the individual qualifies.

Life insurance companies provide financial security for survivors of the insured. A person purchases a life insurance policy by paying **premiums**—prices paid at regular intervals for the policy. Cash collected for premiums on a regular basis builds surplus funds that insurance companies lend to others.

Pension funds are also nonbank financial intermediaries. A **pension** is a regular payment to someone who has worked a certain number of years, reached a certain age, or has suffered an injury. A **pension fund** is a fund that collects and invests funds until the beneficiaries are eligible to receive payments.

Basic Investment Considerations (page 293)

Making Generalizations

As you read, complete the sentence below:

Risky investments can potentially result in high _____ or big _____.

Most investment experts advise savers to understand a few basic principles in order to make good choices among thousands of investment options. The four basic principles include: consistency, simplicity, risk-return relationship, and investment objectives. Successful investors invest consistently over long periods of time. In most cases, the dollar amount invested is not as important as investing regularly.

The risk-return relationship is another important principle. **Risk** is a situation in which the outcome is not certain, but the probabilities can be estimated. Risky investments demand higher returns as compensation. Low risk investments are considered safer because their outcome is easier to predict.

The reason for investing is just as important a consideration as how to invest. Each investor must evaluate their financial goals and needs. The time frame in which investors need to access their savings directly affects the choices they make. For examples, stocks and bonds are better choices for investors who are saving money for retirement, while CDs are a better choice for investors who will need to use the funds within a year or two.

Answer these questions to check your understanding of the entire section.

1. How do individuals benefit from loaning their savings to borrowers?

_____

_____

_____

2. What factors should investors consider when choosing from investment options?

_____

_____

_____

Expository Writing

Write a compare and contrast essay about two investors' financial goals and needs. Compare the goals and needs of an investor who is five years from retirement to an investor who is thirty years from retirement. You may make up details about the investors' income, profession, and assets.

_____

_____

_____

_____

_____

_____

_____

_____

_____

_____

_____

_____

Financial Assets and Their Markets

Big Idea

As you read pages 296–303 in your textbook, complete this graphic organizer by identifying and describing at least four financial assets.

Financial Assets

 **Notes** | **Read to Learn**

Bonds as Financial Assets (page 297)

Predicting

If a bond issuer has a poor credit history, will its bond receive a high rating or a low rating? How will the bond be priced to offset the risk?

_____

_____

_____

Governments or firms issue bonds to borrow funds for long periods of time. A **bond** is a contract to repay borrowed money and interest at regular future intervals. A bond consists of three main parts. The **coupon** is the stated interest on a corporate, municipal, or government bond. The **maturity** is the life of the bond or the length of time that funds are borrowed. The **par value** is the principal of a bond, or the total amount borrowed.

An investor must consider three factors before deciding what bond to buy. One factor is the **current yield,** or the measure of a bond's return. Current yield is the annual coupon interest divided by the purchase price. The other two factors are the issuer's financial health and changes in future interest rates. The price of a bond is also a factor, however, it is ultimately set by supply and demand.

Two major corporations, Moody's and Standard & Poor's, publish bond ratings. Bond ratings are based on the issuer's financial health, ability to make payments, and past credit history. Ratings range from AAA, which is high, to D, which is low. Bonds with higher ratings sell at higher prices than bonds with lower ratings.

 **Notes** | **Read to Learn**

Financial Assets and Their Characteristics *(page 299)*

Synthesizing Information

List the five types of financial assets that are issued by various levels of government.

1. _____

2. _____

3. _____

4. _____

5. _____

Investors can choose from many kinds of financial assets. Certificates of deposit, or CDs, are loans that investors make to financial institutions. Investors can select the CD's maturity.

Corporate bonds provide funds for corporations. **Junk bonds** carry a high rate of return to offset the greater risk of not paying the loans back. Investors usually consider corporate bonds a long-term investment.

State and local governments raise money by issuing **municipal bonds,** or munis. Munis are **tax-exempt,** which means that state governments, the federal government, or both do not tax the interest paid to investors.

There are two types of **savings bonds,** or EE savings bonds. Both are low-denomination bonds issued by the U.S. government. Paper-based bonds are purchased for 50 percent less than their redemption value, and they can be redeemed at full value on a specific date. Paperless bonds sells for their face value and earn interest. Investors can buy these bonds for their heirs by designating a **beneficiary,** who will inherit the ownership of the financial asset when the purchaser dies. Savings bonds cannot be sold to someone else, but they can be redeemed early, with some loss of interest.

The U.S. government offers three other types of investments with varying terms. A **treasury note** has a maturity of two to ten years. A **treasury bond,** on the other hand, has a maturity of ten to thirty years. These financial assets have the lowest return of any investment because they are so safe. A **treasury bill,** or T-bill, sells in increments of $1,000 and has a maturity of one year or less.

Individual retirement accounts, or IRAs, are long-term, tax-sheltered time deposits. Annual contributions are not taxed until they are withdrawn during retirement.

Market for Financial Assets *(page 302)*

Drawing Conclusions

In which market do treasury bonds and treasury notes belong?

_____

Financial assets are grouped into different markets. The **capital market** is for funds loaned for more than one year. The **money market** is for funds loaned for less than one year.

Another way to group assets is by how easily they can be redeemed. In the **primary market,** only the original issuer can repurchase or redeem a financial asset, so it offers less liquidity. In the **secondary market,** on the other hand, financial assets can be sold to someone other than the original issuer. This market offers more liquidity because assets can be redeemed easily without penalty.

 **Answer these questions to check your understanding of the entire section.**

1. What three factors must an investor consider when choosing a bond?

_____

_____

_____

2. Name and describe the four markets used to group financial assets.

_____

_____

_____

Expository Writing

Suppose that you are not wealthy but want your only grandchild to inherit $100,000 at your death. In a letter that your grandchild will receive on his or her 21st birthday, explain what financial assets you have purchased and why. To make your decisions, consider carefully the risk and return of each type of financial asset. Keep in mind that your goal is to leave your grandchild as much money as possible.

_____

_____

_____

_____

_____

_____

_____

_____

_____

_____

_____

Chapter 11, Section 2

Investing in Equities and Options

Big Idea

As you read pages 305–311 in your textbook, use this graphic organizer to describe the different stock markets.

Stock Market	Characteristics
NYSE	

Read to Learn

Stocks and Efficient Markets (page 306)

Problems and Solutions

Describe one strategy an investor could use to decrease the risks of involved when investing in stocks.

_____

_____

_____

_____

_____

_____

Stocks are also called **equities** and are shares of common stocks. One way to buy equities is through a **stockbroker,** a person who buys or sells equities for clients.

The demand for a particular company's stock increases as that company's prospects for growth improve. Growth influences supply and demand, which then affects stock prices. Many stock market experts agree with a theory called **Efficient Market Hypothesis (EMH).** According to this theory, stocks are always priced correctly because they are closely watched. What this means is that the price of all stock has the potential to go up or down. Many investors decrease their risk through **portfolio diversification,** or owning many investments.

Mutual funds and 401(k) plans are popular ways to diversify a portfolio. A **mutual fund** company sells stock in itself and uses the funds to buy stocks and bonds issued by other companies. The **net asset value (NAV)** or market value of a mutual fund share is found by dividing the net value of the fund by the number of shares issued. **401(k) plans** are tax-deferred investments and savings plans that act as a personal pension fund.

Notes

Read to Learn

Stock Markets and Their Performance *(page 308)*

Drawing Conclusions

As you read, complete the sentences below:

1. If a stock's price decreases at a greater rate than the S&P 500, it may signal an investor to _____.

2. If a stock's price decreases during a bear market, it may signal an investor to _____.

Stocks are traded in markets. There are two kinds of markets: organized stock or securities exchanges, and over-the-counter markets. At a **stock exchange** or **securities exchange,** buyers and sellers meet to trade stocks. Trading can take place only on the floor of the exchange. The New York Stock Exchange (NYSE) lists stocks from the largest and most profitable companies. The American Stock Exchange (AMEX), also in New York City, lists smaller and more risky but potentially profitable companies. **Over-the-counter markets** (OTC) are electronic marketplaces for stocks not listed on organized exchanges. An investor who opens an Internet account with a brokerage firm can buy and sell stocks in both markets.

Investors compare the movement of their stocks against popular indicators. One performance indicator is the **Dow Jones Industrial Average (DJIA).** It measures stock market trends based on 30 representative stocks from the NYSE. Another performance indicator is the **Standard & Poor's 500 (S&P 500).** It measures market trends based on 500 stocks from the NYSE, the AMEX, and OTC.

Specific terms are used to describe the market's movement. A **bull market** is a period during which stock market prices move up for several months or years in a row. During a **bear market,** stock market prices move down for several months or years in a row.

Trading in the Future *(page 311)*

Determining Cause and Effect

How do options reduce the risk of buying futures contracts?

Although most securities transactions happen in the present, securities transactions can also take place at a later time. A **spot market** is a market in which a transaction is made immediately at the prevailing price. A **futures contract** is an agreement to buy or sell at a specific date in the future at a predetermined price.

There are two kinds of futures contracts called **options,** which give a buyer the right to cancel the contract. A **call option** is a futures contract giving a buyer the right to cancel a contract to buy something at a specific future price. A **put option** is a futures contract giving a buyer the right to cancel a contract to sell something at a specific future price.

Section Wrap-up

Answer these questions to check your understanding of the entire section.

1. Describe three factors that influence the price of a stock.

_____

_____

_____

2. Which stock transactions are more risky spot market transactions or futures contracts?

_____

_____

_____

Persuasive Writing

Write an essay agreeing or disagreeing with the Efficient Market Hypothesis (EMH). If you agree, try to use examples of public traded corporations that performed in a similar way as other stocks. If you disagree, try to use examples of public traded corporations that performed very differently than other stocks.

_____

_____

_____

_____

_____

_____

_____

_____

_____

_____

_____

_____

Measuring the Nation's Output and Income

Big Idea

As you read pages 319–327 in your textbook, complete this graphic organizer by describing how the different economic sectors contribute to the nation's economic activity.

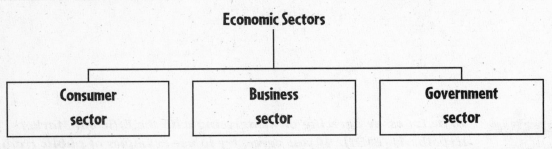

Economic Sectors

- Consumer sector
- Business sector
- Government sector

Notes | Read to Learn

GDP—The Measure of National Output (page 320)

Making Generalizations

As you read, complete the sentence below.

GDP is an indicator of the economy's overall health because it measures _____ in which both parties believe that they will _____ _____ from the transaction.

Economists study several key measures to understand the country's economic health. The branch of economics that considers the economy as a whole is called **macroeconomics.**

Gross domestic product (GDP) is the national output. GDP measures the voluntary transactions that take place in the market. It is found by multiplying the quantity of each good by its price and then adding all of the results. The GDP excludes intermediate products, secondhand sales, nonmarket transactions, and transactions that occur in the underground economy. **Intermediate products** are goods used to make other products already counted. **Secondhand sales** are sales of used goods. **Nonmarket transactions** are economic activities that do not take place in the market. Transactions in the **underground economy** are unreported legal and illegal activities.

There are three measures of the GDP. GDP not adjusted for inflation is the **current GDP.** Economists use a **base year** as a point of comparison for other years to adjust the GDP for inflation, a measure called **real GDP. GDP per capita** is the GDP on a per person basis. It is figured by dividing the GDP by the population.

Read to Learn

GNP—The Measure of National Income *(page 324)*

Analyzing Information

Can you find the DPI if you do not know the PI? Explain.

_____

_____

Economists measure the national income in five ways. **Gross national product (GNP)** is the value of all final goods, services, and structures produced in one year with labor and property supplied by a country's residents, regardless of where the production takes place. **Net national product (NNP),** which is GNP minus depreciation, accounts for wear and tear on capital equipment. **National income (NI)** is NNP minus indirect business taxes, such as excise taxes. **Personal income (PI)** is the total amount of income going to the consumer sector before they pay individual income taxes. **Disposal personal income (DPI)** is personal income less individual income taxes.

Economic Sectors and Circular Flows *(page 325)*

Drawing Conclusions

Which one of the four sectors could have a negative value?

_____

_____

_____

Output generates income that flows through the economy's four sectors. The consumer, or household, sector is the largest. The **household** consists of all persons in a house, apartment, or room. A household can also be an **unrelated individual,** which is a person living alone even though he or she might have family somewhere else. A household can also be a **family,** or a group of two or more people living together who are related by blood, marriage, or adoption. The consumer sector's income is disposable personal income.

The second sector is the investment sector. It receives its income from the retained earnings that are subtracted from NI and the capital consumption allowances that are subtracted from GNP. The third is the government sector. Its income is from various taxes and Social Security contributions. Finally the foreign sector's income represents the difference between the dollar value of goods sent abroad and the dollar value of goods purchased from abroad.

The Output-Expenditure Model *(page 327)*

Determining Cause and Effect

*What will happen to GDP if consumers spend more?*_____

_____

The **output-expenditure model** describes aggregate economic activity by the consumer, investment, government, and foreign sectors. This model specifies how the various sectors spend their money. The model can be represented by the equation

$GDP = C + I + G + (X - M)$. The foreign sector's purchases are called **net exports of goods and services.** They are equal to total exports minus total imports. In the equation, the foreign sector is abbreviated as $X - M$ to reflect the difference between exports (X) and imports (M).

Section Wrap-up

Answer these questions to check your understanding of the entire section.

1. What four things does the GDP exclude? Why?

_____

_____

_____

2. How do economists measure the national income (NI)?

_____

_____

_____

Expository Writing

Suppose that you are an economist who writes a newspaper column that answers readers' questions. This week, your column must answer this question: What are the four economic sectors, and how do they spend and receive their income?

_____

_____

_____

_____

_____

_____

_____

_____

_____

_____

Population and Economic Growth

Big Idea

As you read pages 329–335 in your textbook, complete this graphic organizer by identifying changes in the United States in the listed categories.

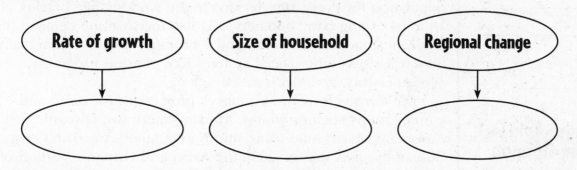

Rate of growth	Size of household	Regional change

Notes	Read to Learn

Population in the United States *(page 330)*

Problems and Solutions

What steps must people take to offset the effects that a growing population has on infrastructure?

_____

_____

Every ten years, the U.S. takes a **census**—a count of population. The census helps to apportion the number of representatives that each state elects to Congress. It also gives useful information about the population.

The Census Bureau classifies its data in several ways. One category is **urban population,** which is all the people who live in incorporated cities, towns, and villages. Another category is **rural population**—people who do not live in urban areas.

The rate of growth has continually declined since colonial times, even though the population itself has increased. Also, since the 1970s, the population of the United States has shifted from the older, industrial North and East toward the warmer, roomier parts of the country. The **center of population**—the point where the country would balance if it were flat and everyone weighed the same—has shifted from Maryland to Missouri.

Population changes affect the country's **infrastructure,** or public goods needed to support a population. To offset how population distorts the GDP, economists measure GDP per capita.

 **Notes** | **Read to Learn**

Projected Population Trends *(page 332)*

Making Inferences

How would business owners use data from the Census Bureau?

_____

_____

_____

_____

_____

Distinguishing Fact from Opinion

*Is the following statement a fact or an opinion? Why?*_____

The Bureau projects that by 2050, the life expectancy will increase to 82.1 years.

Determining Cause and Effect

What are some of the negative economic effects of declining population growth?

_____

_____

_____

_____

The Census Bureau uses the data collected to make projections about how the population will change in the future. One group that the Bureau studies closely is people born during the **baby boom**—the historically high birthrate years in the United States from 1946 to 1964. A **population pyramid,** which shows the breakdown of population by age and gender, shows that baby boomers are a large group of the population. As baby boomers age, they will create changes in the **dependency ratio.** This ratio is the number of children and elderly people in the population for every 100 persons in the working-age bracket of 18 to 64. Aging baby boomers will also increase the demand for medicines, medical facilities, and retirement homes. Additionally, they will stress other social systems like pension programs, Social Security, and Medicare benefits.

The Census Bureau also makes projections for racial and ethnic groups such as whites, African Americans, Hispanic Americans, Asian Americans, and Native Americans. The Census Bureau predicts that by 2050 the Asian and Hispanic portion of the population will nearly double. The African American portion of the population will also increase but not as much.

Demographers state that three major factors affect population growth. **Demographers** are people who study the growth, density, and other characteristics of a population. The first factor is the **fertility rate,** which is the number of births that 1,000 women are expected to undergo in their lifetime. The current projected fertility rate of 2.119 births per woman is slightly above the replacement rate. The second factor is the **life expectancy** or the average remaining life span in years for people who attain a given age. Today, the life expectancy is 75.9 years. The Bureau projects that by 2050, the life expectancy will increase to 82.1 years. The third factor is **net immigration**—the net population change after accounting for people who leave and people who enter a country. Net immigration takes into account both immigrants, people who enter a country, and emigrants, people who leave a country.

After examining these three factors, demographers predict that population growth rate in the United States will continue to decline. The current rate is below one percent.

As mentioned above, an aging population will stress medical and social systems. As young people become a smaller percentage of the population, we will need fewer schools and playgrounds. A market economy, however, can accommodate changes with the least amount of disruption of daily life among all of the types of economies.

Section Wrap-up

Answer these questions to check your understanding of the entire section.

1. How does a changing population affect the GDP, and how do economists cope with that affect?

_____

_____

_____

2. Identify and define the three major factors that affect population growth.

_____

_____

_____

Persuasive Writing

Suppose that you are a demographer who will address your city or town council at its upcoming meeting. Write a speech that outlines which parts of your city's or town's infrastructure the council members should expand and why. Be sure to explain what has affected the city's population growth over the last ten years.

_____

_____

_____

_____

_____

_____

_____

_____

_____

_____

_____

Poverty and the Distribution of Income

Big Idea

As you read pages 337–345 in your textbook, complete this graphic organizer by outlining three explanations for a growing income gap.

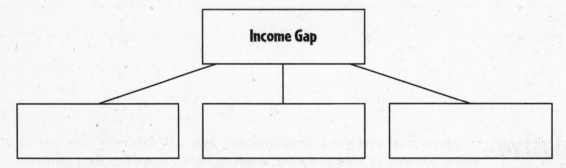

```
                    ┌──────────────────┐
                    │   Income Gap     │
                    └──────────────────┘
         ┌─────────────────┼─────────────────┐
    ┌─────────┐       ┌─────────┐       ┌─────────┐
    │         │       │         │       │         │
    │         │       │         │       │         │
    └─────────┘       └─────────┘       └─────────┘
```

 **Notes**   ## Read to Learn

Poverty (page 338)

Making Inferences

1. Why would inflation be a factor in the calculation of the poverty threshold?

_____

_____

_____

_____

2. Would inflation affect a Lorenz curve? Explain.

_____

_____

Although you are familiar with the word *poverty*, its meaning can be relative. In economics, however, it must be clearly defined. The Social Security Administration sets a **poverty threshold** which is the annual dollar income used to determine the number of people living in poverty. People classified as living in poverty earn less income than the poverty threshold. The government simplifies the poverty thresholds to create **poverty guidelines.** These administrative guidelines help to determine eligibility for certain federal programs.

Economists analyze how income is distributed among households by ranking household incomes by quintiles, or fifths. Next, economists calculate the total amount of the nation's income that each quintile earns.

A **Lorenz curve** shows the distribution of income between households, occupations, or individuals. Economists draw a household Lorenz curve by plotting and connecting the quintiles' data points on a graph. In recent years, the curve is widening towards the bottom and the right which tells us that the income gap between quintiles is increasing.

Read to Learn

Reasons for Income Inequality *(page 340)*

Determining Cause and Effect

Explain one other way that wealth can increase the income of individuals.

_____

_____

_____

People's incomes vary widely for many reasons. Education is one of the most important reasons. People with higher levels of education earn more money. A person with a college degree earns almost twice as much as a person with a high-school diploma.

The gap between the distribution of wealth in the United States is much greater than the gap between the distribution of income. When economists rank people by their wealth, the top quintile holds 75 percent of all the wealth in the country. On the other hand, the bottom two-fifths hold less than two percent of the nation's wealth. This worsens the income gap of the next generation because children of the wealthy can attend expensive universities or colleges and can be set up in businesses where they will earn a large income.

Other reasons for the income gap include tax law changes, the decline of unions, the increase in service jobs, monopoly power, discrimination, and an increase in single-parent families.

Antipoverty Programs *(page 342)*

Formulating Questions

Before you read this passage, write two questions you think the text will answer.

1. _____

_____

2. _____

_____

The federal government tries to help the needy. Most government assistance programs fall under the heading of **welfare**—economic and social assistance from the government or private agencies. Despite the intention of welfare programs, reducing poverty has been difficult.

Assistance from the federal government comes in many forms. Income assistance programs provide cash directly to those in need. General assistance programs assist people in other ways. **Food stamps,** for example, are government-issued coupons that can be redeemed for food. Another general assistance program is **Medicaid.** This is a joint federal-state medical insurance program for low-income people.

Tax programs are another way to provide assistance. The most popular is the **Earned Income Tax Credit (EITC).** It provides tax credits and even cash to low-income workers. The **negative income tax** is a proposed type of tax that would make cash payments to certain groups below the poverty line. The program, not available today, could replace welfare programs.

State governments provide and have some control over assistance programs as well. Many offer social services. Some have created **enterprise zones** where companies can locate free of taxes. Rising welfare costs have led state and local governments to require labor from welfare recipients. These **workfare** recipients often assist law enforcement officials or highway crews.

Section Wrap-up

Answer these questions to check your understanding of the entire section.

1. What is the purpose of the poverty threshold?

_____

_____

_____

2. Why are some governments using workfare programs? What advantages are offered by these types of programs?

_____

_____

_____

Informative Writing

Suppose you live in neighborhood which you believe would greatly benefit from being designated as an enterprise zone. Write a letter to your mayor and city council describing the features of the neighborhood which makes it a good candidate for the enterprise zone program. You may make up details to support your main ideas.

_____

_____

_____

_____

_____

_____

_____

_____

_____

_____

_____

_____

Business Cycles and Fluctuations

Big Idea

As you read pages 353–359 in your textbook, complete this graphic organizer by filling in factors that can cause changes in the business cycle.

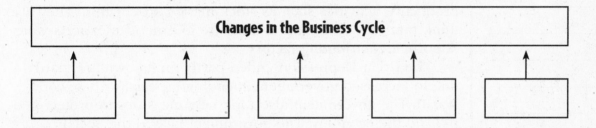

Changes in the Business Cycle

↑   ↑   ↑   ↑   ↑

☐   ☐   ☐   ☐   ☐

Notes | Read to Learn

Business Cycles: Characteristics and Causes *(page 354)*

Synthesizing Information

As you read, complete the sentence below.

You can measure a business cycle from peak to _____ to peak, which includes a _____ and a period of _____.

Both **business cycles**—regular increases and decreases in real GDP, and **business fluctuations**—irregular increases and decreases in real GDP, interrupt economic growth.

Two phases, recession and expansion, mark a business cycle. **Recession,** a decline in real GDP for two quarters, begins when the economy reaches a **peak,** the point the real GDP stops expanding, and ends at a **trough,** the point the real GDP stops declining. After this, the economy enters **expansion,** a continuous period of growth in real GDP. If the economy does not experience recession or expansion, it follows a growth path called a **trend line.** A recession may also become a **depression** characterized by high unemployment, declining real incomes, and overcapacity in manufacturing plants.

There are several causes of business cycles. Capital expenditures, an innovation relating to a product or task, monetary policy decisions by the Federal Reserve System affecting interest rates, and external shocks, such as changes in energy costs, may cause business cycles, as may several factors working together.

Business Cycles in the United States *(page 356)*

Formulating Questions

Before you read about business cycles in the U.S., list two questions you think this passage will answer.

1. _____

_____

_____

2. _____

_____

_____

The Great Depression was the worst economic downturn in U.S. history. Between 1929 and 1933, real GDP declined nearly 50 percent, 12.8 million people were out of work, and the average manufacturing wage fell from 55 cents to 5 cents an hour. Many banks failed. The size of the money supply fell by one-third, so people paid public workers with **depression scrip,** unofficial currency issued by local government bodies.

Economists think the Great Depression occurred because of the wide gap in distribution of income. Poor workers did not have income to spend while the rich used their income on non-productive activities such as stock market speculation. They also think that easy credit and a decrease in American exports were important contributing factors.

The Great Depression ended partly on its own and partly due to increased government spending especially after World War II. The government also took new measures to protect people and the economy. The government passed the Social Security Act of 1935, introduced minimum wage and unemployment programs, established the Securities and Exchange Commission (SEC), and created the Federal Deposit Insurance Corporation (FDIC).

After World War II, business cycles were more moderate; recessions averaged 10 months while expansions averaged 54 months. After the early 1980s, recessions were fewer, and record-setting expansion occurred during the Reagan and the Clinton administrations.

Forecasting Business Cycles *(page 358)*

Making Inferences

Why do economists combine individual series in the LEI?

_____

_____

_____

_____

_____

Economists can use statistical series or macroeconomic models to predict business cycles. For example, they might use a **leading economic indicator,** which is a statistical series that shows a change before the economy changes in a similar way. Or they might use a **composite index of leading economic indicators (LEI),** which combines ten individual statistical series, to predict economic turning points. On average, the time from when an index drops to a recession is nine months, and from when the indicators rise to an expansion is four months.

Another way economists forecast business cycles is by using an **econometric model,** a mathematical expression describing the expected performance of the economy. Most models start with the output-expenditure model, $GDP = C + I + G + (X - M)$. In time, predicted changes are compared to the actual changes in the economy.

Section Wrap-up

Answer these questions to check your understanding of the entire section.

1. Explain what happens at the beginning and the end of a recession.

_____

_____

_____

2. List five government reforms created in response to the Great Depression.

_____

_____

_____

Informative Writing

Write an article for your school newspaper explaining the peaks and troughs of the business cycle and how teens can benefit from monitoring the cycle. Discuss how different phases of the business cycle affect employment, car loans, and small businesses.

_____

_____

_____

_____

_____

_____

_____

_____

_____

_____

_____

Inflation

Big Idea

As you read pages 361–367 in your textbook, complete this graphic organizer by describing the steps in a wage-price spiral.

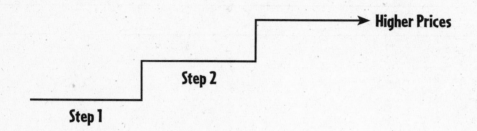

Higher Prices

Step 2

Step 1

Notes | Read to Learn

Measuring Prices and Inflation (page 362)

Drawing Conclusions

The period of rising prices and high unemployment in the United States in the 70s is an example of which kind of inflation?

Economists measure inflation through a **price index,** which measure changes in the price level over time. **Inflation** occurs when the general level of prices of goods and services increases, while **deflation** occurs when the price level decreases. The most popular measure is the **consumer price index (CPI).** In order to compile a CPI, first select a **market basket** that represents commonly purchased goods and services. Then, find the average price of each item and select a **base year** from which to compare all other years. Finally, convert the dollar cost of the market basket into an index value by dividing the cost of every market basket by the base-year market basket cost.

To measure inflation, divide the change in the CPI by the beginning value of the CPI. Today the U.S. has **creeping inflation**—low inflation in the range of 1 to 3 percent. Sometimes inflation can soar, causing **hyperinflation** in the range of 500 percent or more a year. A period of slow economic growth and inflation is called **stagflation**.

Economists also use the **producer price index (PPI)**—to measure prices domestic producers receive—and the **implicit GDP price deflator**—to measure price changes in the GDP.

Causes of Inflation (page 365)

Problems and Solutions

How can the Fed control inflation?

_____

_____

_____

_____

Almost every period of inflation is caused by either one or a combination of the following: a demand-pull inflation, cost-push inflation, wage-price spiral, and/or excessive money growth. According to the **demand-pull inflation** theory, prices rise because all sectors of the economy try to buy more goods and services than the economy can produce. Excessive demand creates shortages that pull prices up. The **cost-push inflation** theory claims that rising input costs, especially energy and organized labor, drive up the prices of products. This leads manufacturers to recover increased costs by raising prices. The wage-price spiral, on the other hand, explains that rising prices do not result from a particular group or event but is instead a self-maintaining spiral of wages and prices that is difficult to stop. The spiral may begin when higher prices make workers demand higher wages, which leads to producers trying to recover that cost with higher prices. Excessive monetary growth—when the money supply grows faster than real GDP—is the most popular explanation for inflation. A demand-pull effect that drives up prices occurs when people spend the additional money created by the Federal Reserve System. Advocates of this explanation believe that a growing money supply maintains inflation.

Consequences of Inflation (page 366)

Making Inferences

Why might a person who is working cope with inflation better than a retired person on a fixed income?

_____

_____

_____

_____

_____

High inflation can reduce purchasing power, distort spending, encourage speculation, and affect the distribution of income. Inflation reduces consumers' purchasing power because the dollar buys less as prices rise. In this way, the dollar loses value over time. The reduced purchasing power of the dollar is especially hard for people with fixed incomes, such as retirees.

When prices rise, distorted spending patterns emerge because people use their money differently. For example, when there has been a rise in interest rates in the past, spending on durable goods has fallen dramatically. Inflation also encourages speculation. People may try to take advantage of rising prices by investing in ventures with higher risks. However, such investments can lose money, and the average consumer usually can't absorb heavy losses. Finally, inflation can distort the distribution of income. During periods of long inflation, a **creditor,** a person or institution who lends money, is generally hurt more, because the **debtor,** a person who borrows and therefore owes money, pays the earlier loan back with dollars that buy less.

1. Name three statistical series economists use to measure inflation. Which series is the most popular?

_____

_____

_____

2. Name and describe the four consequences of inflation.

_____

_____

_____

Descriptive Writing

Suppose that you are living in a country that is experiencing a period of hyperinflation. Write a short story in which you describe a scene at a town market as you try to make purchases to meet your basic needs.

_____

_____

_____

_____

_____

_____

_____

_____

_____

_____

_____

_____

Unemployment

Big Idea

As you read pages 369–375 in your textbook, complete this graphic organizer by filling in the different sources of unemployment.

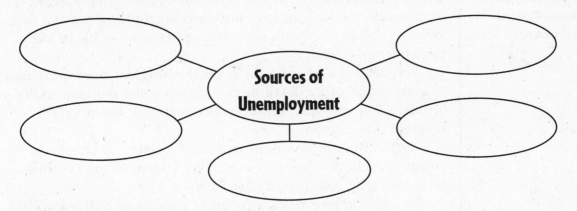

Sources of Unemployment

 **Notes** | # Read to Learn

Measuring Unemployment (page 370)

Predicting

As you read, complete the sentence below.

If the number of unemployed people remained the same and the number of people in the civilian labor force increased, the unemployment rate would _____.

Measuring the unemployment rate is difficult and politically charged. First, we must find the size of the **civilian labor force.** It includes people 16 and over who are either working or looking for a job, and it excludes members of the military and persons in jails or mental health facilities. Then we measure the **unemployed,** people working for less than one hour per week for pay or profit in a non-family owned business, while being available and having made an effort to find a job during the past month. People are also unemployed if they worked in a family business without pay for less than 15 hours a week.

The **unemployment rate** is the number of unemployed persons divided by the total number of persons in the civilian labor force. It is expressed as a percentage of the entire **labor force.** In general, the unemployment rate rises just before a recession begins and rises sharply during the recession.

The unemployment rate understates unemployment, however, because it does not measure *underemployment*. It does not count people who want to work but who are too frustrated to look for a job. It also considers part-time workers fully employed.

Sources of Unemployment (page 372)

Determining Cause and Effect

Describe the effect of technology as it relates to structural unemployment and technological unemployment.

_____

_____

_____

_____

There are several kinds of unemployment. Some kinds are easier to remedy than others. **Frictional employment** involves workers changing jobs or waiting to start new ones. There is always some frictional unemployment since there are always workers changing jobs.

Structural unemployment is more serious. It occurs when a fundamental change in the economy reduces the demand for some workers. For example, **outsourcing**—hiring outside firms to more cheaply perform non-core operations—adds to structural unemployment.

Technological change causes **technological unemployment.** It is the result of automation that makes some workers' skills obsolete. For example, online services reduce the need for regional salespersons.

Cyclical unemployment is directly related to swings in the business cycle. It takes place over the course of the business cycle and may last three to five years.

Changes in the weather or other conditions that reduce the demand for jobs cause **seasonal unemployment.** For example, beach lifeguards in the Northeast are only hired during the summer months. Seasonal unemployment takes place every year, regardless of the economy's health.

Costs of Instability (page 374)

Synthesizing Information

As you read, complete the sentence below.

When GDP declines, the size of the GDP gap

_____

and the misery index

_____.

Fears about recession, inflation, and unemployment are justified because economic instability has great costs—such as personal anxiety or divorce in families.

Unemployment means that fewer goods and services are produced. The **GDP gap** is the difference between what the economy can and does produce. The gap is a kind of opportunity cost. It is a measure of the output not produced because of unused resources. Even a fraction of a percentage point decline in GDP can mean an enormous loss of production and income.

The **misery index,** or **discomfort index,** is the sum of the monthly inflation and unemployment rates. It is an unofficial index that provides a reasonable measure of consumer suffering during high inflation and unemployment.

Uncertainty exists in an unstable economy. All sectors of the economy may decide to spend less thereby causing more unemployment, possibly raising prices, and reducing government services. Political instability also occurs because dissatisfied voters may vote incumbents out of office or vote for radical change. Economic instability also leads to rises in crime and poverty.

Section Wrap-up

Answer these questions to check your understanding of the entire section.

1. How is the monthly unemployment rate expressed?

_____

_____

_____

2. What are two ways that cyclical unemployment is different than seasonal unemployment?

_____

_____

_____

Expository Writing

Write a cause and effect essay that explains which kind of unemployment negatively affects teens looking for work in the summer.

_____

_____

_____

_____

_____

_____

_____

_____

_____

_____

_____

_____

The Evolution, Functions, and Characteristics of Money

Big Idea

As you read pages 383–388 in your textbook, complete this graphic organizer by filling in the characteristics of money.

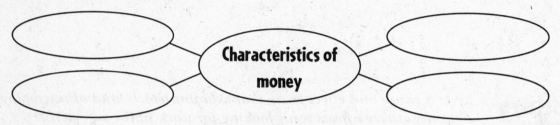

Characteristics of money

Notes

Read to Learn

The Evolution of Money *(page 384)*

Problems and Solutions

How did money solve the problems of a barter economy?

_____

_____

_____

Before the invention of money, more than 4,000 years ago, people bartered, or exchanged goods. In a **barter economy,** trade can only occur if both people want exactly what the other person has and if both people are willing to trade what they have. A barter economy relies on a "mutual coincidence of wants." As a result, transactions are difficult.

The invention of money provided a solution to a barter economy. Primitive societies used **commodity money**—shells, animal hides, or even butter. Such items had an alternative use as an economic good, or commodity, and people decided that it had a certain value. Later, people used **fiat money,** or money that has value by government decree.

Early settlers in America used many forms of money including commodity money and fiat money. Paper money was printed to fund the Revolutionary War. Colonists also used small amounts of **specie,** or money in the form of gold or silver coins. The most popular specie was the Spanish peso. In the United States, dollars eventually became the **monetary unit,** or the standard unit of currency.

Notes | Read to Learn

Characteristics and Functions of Money (page 386)

Identifying the Main Idea

Write the main idea of the first paragraph below in your own words.

_____

_____

_____

Comparing and Contrasting

How are M1 and M2 similar?

_____

_____

_____

_____

How are they different?

_____

_____

_____

_____

What can be used as money? Anything that is portable, durable, divisible, and limited in supply. Modern money and ancient money share the same characteristics. It is important that money is *portable* so that it can be easily transferred from one person to another. Money must also be *durable* so that it does not fall apart when people handle it. It must also be *divisible*, or easily broken into smaller units. Lastly, it must be available in a *limited supply* because money loses its value if too much exists.

Money fills three roles in an economy. For one thing, money is a **medium of exchange,** which means that it is generally accepted as payment for goods and services. If most people accept something as being valuable, then that something can be used as money.

The second role of money in an economy is as a **measure of value,** or a common way to express value. We all know what dollars and cents are, so we measure value in dollars and cents.

The final role of money is as a **store of value.** By storing value money allows time to pass between exchanges. People can store purchasing power until they need it.

Today, the **Federal Reserve System** (the Fed) issues most of our money. The Fed is the privately owned, publicly controlled central bank of the United States. The Fed issues **Federal Reserve Notes** (paper currency).

Federal Reserve notes and metallic coins are two kinds of modern money. A third type is **demand deposit accounts (DDA)** which are accounts from which money can be removed by writing a check and without having to gain prior approval from the depository institution. Because there are different kinds of money, the Fed divided the money supply into two groups: M1 and M2. **M1** includes forms of money that function as a medium of exchange. Checking accounts, coins and currency, DDAs, and traveler's checks belong to M1. **M2** includes the forms of money that function as a store of value. As a result all of M1 also belongs to M2 along with M2 money market funds, savings deposits, and time deposits.

Section Wrap-up

Answer these questions to check your understanding of the entire section.

1. Why would specie be more desirable than fiat or commodity money?

_____

_____

_____

2. Which of the following would be the best choice for commodity money: dried fruit, pine cones, or sea glass? Explain.

_____

_____

_____

Descriptive Writing

Write a short fiction story about a merchant in ancient times that illustrates the difficulties faced in a barter economy.

_____

_____

_____

_____

_____

_____

_____

_____

_____

_____

_____

_____

The Development of Modern Banking

Big Idea

As you read pages 390–397 in your textbook, complete this time line by listing major events in U.S. monetary history in the appropriate spaces.

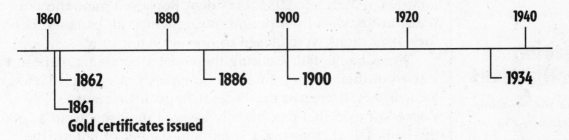

1860   1880   1900   1920   1940

   1862   1886   1900   1934

1861
Gold certificates issued

 **Notes** | **Read to Learn**

The Development of Banking in America (page 391)

Analyzing Information

What problems occurred when the banking services provided by state banks were not regulated?

_____

_____

_____

_____

The U.S. Constitution allowed private banks to issue paper currency, which state banks printed in local print shops after the Revolution. A **state bank** is a bank that receives its charter from the state where it operates. Neither federal nor state governments regulated the money supply. When the Civil War began in 1861, Congress printed money for the first time since the adoption of the Constitution. The currency was **legal tender,** or fiat currency.

In 1863, Congress reformed the banking system with the National Currency Act. The act created a National Banking System (NBS) made up of **national banks,** which receive their operating charters from the federal government. The banks issued **national currency**—currency backed by government bonds. A few years later, the federal government placed a tax on privately-issued bank notes and state banks withdrew them.

From 1863 to 1934, the government issued **gold certificates**, or paper currency backed by gold. Additionally, between 1878 and 1968, the government issued **silver certificates**, which were paper currency backed by and redeemable for silver.

Notes

Read to Learn

The Creation of the Fed (page 394)

Determining Cause and Effect

What events led to the creation of the FDIC?

_____

_____

_____

Making Generalizations

What is the relationship between the reserve requirements and the money supply?

_____

_____

_____

_____

Underline the facts in the passage that support your statement.

Congress again reformed the nation's banking system in 1913 with the creation of the Federal Reserve System. Congress created the Fed as the nation's **central bank,** a bank that can lend money to other banks. All national banks were required to become members, and all state banks were eligible to join. The banks that joined bought shares of stock in the system.

When the Depression began in 1929, many banks failed. Some experienced a **bank run,** or a sudden rush by depositors to withdraw all deposited funds in anticipation of the bank's failure. On March 5, 1933, President Roosevelt announced a **bank holiday**—a brief period during which all banks or depository institutions were closed to prevent bank runs.

When banks failed during the Great Depression, depositors lost all of their money. In 1933, Congress passed the Glass-Steagall Act. It created the Federal Deposit Insurance Corporation (FDIC) that initially insured deposits up to $2,500 if the bank failed. Today, if a bank is in danger of failing, the FDIC can seize it and either sell it to a stronger bank or liquidate it to pay off its depositors. Either way, the customers get their money. Currently, the FDIC insures accounts up to $100,000.

As checking accounts became popular in the last century, the Fed developed other important banking practices including the **fractional reserve system.** It requires financial institutions to set aside only a fraction of their deposits in the form of legal reserves. **Legal reserves** are coins and currency that banks hold in their vaults or deposits at the Fed. The **reserve requirement** dictates the size of a bank's reserves. This is a percentage of every deposit that must be set aside as legal reserves. All other funds made available to borrowers are called **excess reserves.** As a result, banks are able to circulate a greater amount of funds than they hold in reserve, thereby multiplying the money supply. For example, suppose you open a checking or DDA with an opening deposit of $5,000 and the current reserve requirement is 20 percent. The bank must hold $1,000 of the $5,000 deposit in reserves in their vault or at the **member bank reserve (MBR).** Then suppose the bank lends the remaining $4,000 to your neighbor, Ernie, to renovate his kitchen. He can receive the loan in cash or in the form of a DDA. If Ernie receives the $4,000 loan in the form of a DDA, the bank must keep 20 percent of his deposit, $800, in MBR. The bank then has $3,200 in excess reserves to loan to others. This money supply expansion continues as long as banks have excess reserves and people deposit their money in bank accounts.

Section Wrap-up

Answer these questions to check your understanding of the entire section.

1. What was the result of Congress passing the National Currency Act and creating the National Banking System?

_____

_____

_____

2. Why is it important for people to trust banks and have DDA accounts?

_____

_____

_____

Informative Writing

Write a blog entry in which you discuss all the features of modern day banking and transactions which people take for granted. Support your opinions and observations by citing facts from Sections 1 and 2.

_____

_____

_____

_____

_____

_____

_____

_____

_____

_____

_____

_____

The Federal Reserve System and Monetary Policy

Big Idea

As you read pages 399–407 in your textbook, complete this graphic organizer by describing the features of the Federal Reserve System.

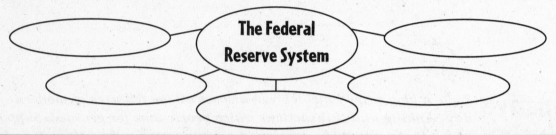

The Federal Reserve System

 **Notes**

Read to Learn

Structure of the Fed *(page 400)*

Problems and Solutions

How does the structure of the Fed help ensure that it acts in the public's interest?

_____

_____

The **member banks** of the Federal Reserve System privately own it. The system requires national banks to belong to the Fed. State banks can choose whether or not to join. It is commonly said that the Fed is "privately owned, but publicly controlled."

A seven-member Board of Governors directs the Fed. The president appoints the members to 14-year terms. The board regulates member banks' operations and makes policies that affect interest rates and the availability of credit.

Twelve district banks provide services such as lending money to privately owned banks.

The Federal Open Market Committee (FOMC) consists of twelve voting members, seven are from the Board of Governors. The FOMC meets eight times a year to evaluate the economy. It makes decisions that directly affect credit.

The Fed also consists of three advisory committees: the Federal Advisory Council, the Consumer Advisory Council, and the Thrift Institutions Advisory Council. They provide advice to the Fed regarding the health of the economy, consumer credit laws, and the savings and loan industry.

Conducting Monetary Policy (page 402)

Predicting

Suppose that inflation was rising rapidly. What step could the Fed take to try curb inflation?

_____

_____

Synthesizing Information

As you read, complete the sentence below.

Through changing the reserve requirement and open market operations, the Fed indirectly affects interest rates while through changing the _____ the Fed directly affects interest rates.

One of the Fed's key functions is to conduct **monetary policy.** This refers to short-run changes in the availability and cost of credit to influence the general level of economic activity. This policy is based on supply and demand. More money, for example, will be demanded when the **interest rate**—or the price of credit to a borrower—is low. The Fed changes interest rates by changing the size of the money supply. Under an **easy money policy,** the Fed expands the money supply. This causes interest rates to fall. Under a **tight money policy,** the Fed limits the money supply. This drives interest rates up.

The Fed has three primary tools to set monetary policy. The reserve requirement is the first tool. The Fed can change the percentage of checking, time, and savings accounts that banks must retain. The balance can then be loaned out by the bank. The Fed rarely changes the reserve requirement although it is a powerful tool.

The Fed's second tool is **open market operations**—the buying and selling of government securities. When the Fed buys securities, more money becomes available to lend. More lending means an increase in the money supply. The reverse occurs when the Fed sells securities.

As a central bank, the Fed lends money to other banks. This provides the Fed with its third monetary tool, the **discount rate.** This rate is interest that the Fed charges on loans to financial institutions. Changes in the discount rate also affect the **prime rate**—the lowest rate of interest that commercial banks charge their best customers.

The effect of these tools on the economy is complex. If the Fed allows the money supply to expand for too long, it can lead to inflation. This is the **quantity theory of money.**

Other Fed Responsibilities (page 406)

Making Inferences

How do truth-in-lending disclosures affect consumers' economic decisions?

_____

_____

The Fed has a number of other responsibilities. **Currency** is made up of Federal Reserve notes. The Bureau of the Mint produces **coins.** The Fed also ensures that various payment systems work smoothly.

The Fed establishes guidelines that govern banking behavior. The Fed also has jurisdiction over the operations of **bank holding companies**—firms that own and control other banks.

The Fed is responsible for some consumer legislation. Under **Regulation Z,** the Fed has the authority to extend truth-in-lending disclosures to consumers. The Fed also provides many financial services to the federal government.

Section Wrap-up

Answer these questions to check your understanding of the entire section.

1. How are the Board of Governor and the Federal Open Market Committee similar and different from each other?

_____

_____

_____

2. In what ways can the Fed stimulate or slow economic growth?

_____

_____

_____

Persuasive Writing

If you were on the FOMC today, would you advocate a tight monetary policy or a loose monetary policy? Write an essay stating your position and use facts, such as the housing market, the unemployment rate, and current interest rates, to support your position.

_____

_____

_____

_____

_____

_____

_____

_____

_____

_____

_____

Macroeconomic Equilibrium

Big Idea

As you read pages 413–417 in your textbook, complete this graphic organizer by filling in at least three factors that could lower production costs and lead to an increase in aggregate supply.

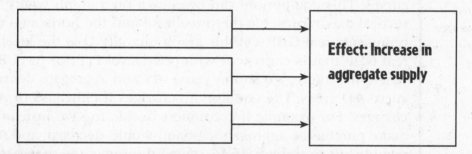

Effect: Increase in aggregate supply

 **Notes** | **Read to Learn**

Aggregate Supply and Demand (page 414)

Determining Cause and Effect

1. How would an increase in the minimum wage most likely affect aggregate demand?

_____

_____

_____

2. How would it affect the aggregate demand curve?

_____

_____

When economists study the whole economy, known as **macroeconomics,** they analyze aggregate supply and demand to see how the **equilibrium price** and quantity of output are determined. **Aggregate supply** is the total value of all products that all firms would produce in a specific period of time at various price levels. To see how price affects real GDP, economists plot an **aggregate supply curve,** a hypothetical curve showing different levels of real GDP produced at various price levels. Economists plot price levels on the vertical axis which shows the prices of *everything* produced. They plot the real GDP on the horizontal axis. It is the value of *all* goods and services produced. The curve slopes upward to the right and certain factors shift the whole curve to the right or the left. Lower production costs shift the curve to the right.

    Aggregate demand is the total value of products demanded at all price levels. The **aggregate demand curve** shows different levels of real GDP that would be bought at various price levels. It slopes downward to the right. Increases in aggregate demand shift the whole curve right and vice versa.

Macroeconomic Equilibrium (page 416)

Aggregate supply and demand curves provide a framework that helps us evaluate how effectively economic policy proposals on economic growth and price stability meet their goals. The curves also help us predict how the economy will change. Although the predictions are not exact, the curves provide a useful way to analyze macroeconomic issues such as macroeconomic equilibrium.

Macroeconomic equilibrium is the point at which the level of real GDP is consistent with a given price level. That point is marked by the intersection of the aggregate supply and demand curves. This equilibrium can be shown on a graph where the vertical axis represents the price level and the horizontal axis represents real GDP. On this graph quantity **Q** is the level of real GDP that is consistent with price level **P.** Price level **P** is where the aggregate supply curve **AS** and aggregate demand curve **AD** cross. The equilibrium changes if either **AS** or **AD** changes. For example if consumers decide to save instead of make purchases, aggregate demand would decrease and **AD** would shift to the left. If **AS** stayed the same, the macroeconomic equilibrium would take place at a lower level of real GDP and price level.

Just as the actions of businesses and consumers can shift either AS or AD curves to the left or the right so can the government's fiscal and monetary policies. Policy makers, therefore, must consider how their decisions will affect macroeconomic equilibrium. For example, if a new government policy caused **AD** to shift to the right, the new equilibrium would be at a higher level of both real GDP and price level. This is one reason policy makers study the curves—they want to make good decisions which result in making real GDP grow without unnecessarily increasing the price level. This would lead to higher inflation.

Section Wrap-up *Answer these questions to check your understanding of the entire section.*

1. How does a graph of an aggregate supply curve differ from a graph of an aggregate demand curve?

_____

_____

_____

2. When is macroeconomic equilibrium reached? How is this shown on a graph?

_____

_____

_____

Expository Writing *Suppose you are hired to speak to newly elected congresspersons about economics. Write a speech that defines aggregate supply, aggregate demand, and macroeconomic equilibrium. Explain why it is important for congresspersons to understand these concepts.*

_____

_____

_____

_____

_____

_____

_____

_____

_____

_____

_____

Chapter 15, Section 1

Stabilization Policies

Big Idea

As you read pages 419–427 in your textbook, complete this graphic organizer by describing the role of government under demand-side and supply-side policies.

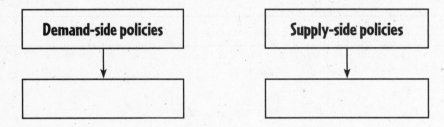

Demand-side policies		Supply-side policies

Notes   Read to Learn

Demand-Side Policies (page 420)

Making Inferences

How does the progressive income tax function as an automatic stabilizer?

_____

_____

_____

_____

_____

_____

_____

_____

      The economist John Maynard Keynes suggested fiscal policies that would lower unemployment by stimulating aggregate demand. A **fiscal policy** is the use of government spending and tax measures to influence the economy. Some are based on **Keynesian economics,** based on the fact that the investment sector is the most unstable of all sectors of the GDP. The effect of the investment sector on the GDP is called the **multiplier** because a change in investment spending causes a magnified effect on total spending. The **accelerator** effect worsens these conditions as changes in total spending changes investment spending.

      Keynes concluded that only the government sector is big enough to counteract this instability. The government should spend funds or reduce taxes to balance changes in the investment sector. After an economic recovery, the government would cut spending or increase taxes to repay the deficit.

      The government's most effective fiscal policy is the **automatic stabilizer,** which offsets a change in people's incomes. An **entitlement,** such as **unemployment insurance** or **Medicare,** and progressive income tax are automatic stabilizers.

Read to Learn

Supply-Side Policies (page 423)

Analyzing Information

What important point is not a consideration of supply-side policies?

_____

_____

_____

_____

Supply-side policies are economic policies designed to stimulate the economy by increasing production. Both demand- and supply-side policies have the same goal: increasing production and employment without increasing inflation.

Supply-siders want to reduce the government's role in the economy by reducing the number of federal agencies, by reducing federal spending, and through deregulation. **Deregulation** is the relaxation or removal of government regulations on business activities. Supply-siders also believe lower tax rates will increase individual productivity. This would increase consumer spending, business activity, and government revenues. Supply-side policies aim to increase production at every price level. This would cause the aggregate supply curve to shift to the right, the real GDP to rise, and the price level to decrease.

Limitations of supply-side policies include a lack of experience to understand how they really affect the economy and a failure to produce the higher tax revenues predicted by the Laffer curve. The goal of these policies is to stimulate economic growth, not economic stability. As a result, they may weaken automatic stabilizers in place.

Monetary Policies (page 426)

Problems and Solutions

What economic problem is not effectively addressed by monetary policy? Why not?

_____

_____

_____

_____

_____

Monetarism stresses the importance of stable monetary growth to control inflation and stimulate long-term economic growth. A contractionary monetary policy works to tighten the money supply. It raises interest rates in the short run to slow consumer and business borrowing. It also shifts the aggregate demand curve to the left and lowers both real GDP and the price level. An expansionary policy works to increase the money supply. In the short run, it lowers interest rates to increase borrowing and shifts the aggregate demand curve right. This causes real GDP and the price level to rise. In the long run, however, expansionary monetary policy might increase inflation. Monetarists, therefore recommend that the money supply should grow at a slow but steady rate determined by the rates of growth of real GDP and productivity. In the 1970s, President Nixon tried to control inflation through **wage-price controls** which made it illegal for firms to give raises or increase prices without government permission. It failed.

Results of monetary policy may happen in the short run or only in the long run. It must also be used carefully because its short-run impacts are uncertain, and monetary policy is unable to reduce short-term unemployment.

Section Wrap-up

Answer these questions to check your understanding of the entire section.

1. Explain how the effect of a successful demand-side policy on real GDP and the price level differs from the effect of a successful supply-side policy.

_____

_____

_____

2. What is the difference between contractionary monetary policy and expansionary monetary policy?

_____

_____

_____

Persuasive Writing

Suppose you are a senator who represents a region where many businesses and homes have been destroyed by a natural disaster. Write a speech that advocates spending federal dollars on public works projects and providing government incentives for investment in the region as good fiscal policy.

_____

_____

_____

_____

_____

_____

_____

_____

_____

_____

_____

Economics and Politics

Big Idea

As you read pages 429–433 in your textbook, complete this graphic organizer by identifying and describing the different kinds of fiscal policy.

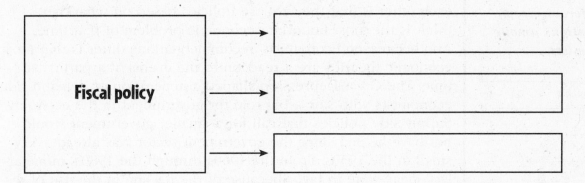

Fiscal policy

Notes   Read to Learn

Changing Nature of Economic Policy (page 430)

Determining Cause and Effect

What historical trend led to the rise of monetary policy?

_____

_____

_____

_____

Government fiscal policies use taxing and spending to speed up or slow down economic growth. *Discretionary* fiscal policies require action by Congress, the president, or a federal agency. *Passive* fiscal policies react automatically when the economy changes. *Structural* fiscal policies are meant to strengthen the economy over a longer period of time. Welfare reform of 1996, for example, made the program financially secure and for most recipients ended the cycle of dependency by providing resources to encourage self-sufficiency.

Discretionary fiscal policy was once the most popular kind. Today, it is much less common because people realize that there are lags between recognizing a problem and solving it. It is also uncommon as a result of inaction, which occurs when political parties in Congress oppose each other's fiscal proposals. Finally it is uncommon because of current ideology, or beliefs that steer policy.

The Federal Reserve System has stepped in while discretionary fiscal policy has decreased. In 2001 through **monetary policy,** the Fed actively lowered the discount rate to stimulate the economy. It worked, and the 2001 recession was short and mild.

 **Notes** | **Read to Learn**

Economics and Politics Today (page 432)

Formulating Questions

Write a question that will help you organize your thoughts about the discussion of different recommendations among economists.

_____

_____

_____

_____

_____

_____

Drawing Conclusions

As you read, underline the facts that support the following conclusion.

In the near future, economists will have to develop policies that help the elderly or help them stay in the workforce for a longer period of time.

The economic conditions of the time shape the recommendations of economists and policymakers. In the 1800s, economics was known as "political economics." Then economists broke away to establish economics as its own science. Today the two fields have come back together to form "economic politics"— politicians concerned with economic effects of their actions.

One reason that economists' recommendations differ from each other is that they choose policies based on what they think is the most important economic problem of that time. Another reason economists' recommendations differ is that most economic theories are a reaction to the events at a particular time. The Great Depression shaped a generation of demand-side economists who saw a big role for government in the economy. Supply-side policies that call for a smaller government would not have helped since the government sector was already very small in the 1930s. From the 1960s through the 1980s, monetarists' ideas were in favor because of the decline in the use of discretionary fiscal policy. By the 1980s, ideology called for the rejection of "big government," which led to the rise of supply-siders who thought smaller government was the key to economic growth. By 2010 the large numbers of retired **baby boomers,** who were born in the United States during the high birthrate years between 1946 and 1964, will have their own issues to confront. Economists will have to address new problems anticipated to arise as this population ages.

Politicians and economists work closely together to steer the economy. The economists advise, while the politicians direct or execute the strategies. The president has the **Council of Economic Advisers,** a three-member group that makes strategies and advises the president on economic matters. Although the president listens to the council's advice, he may not want or be able to follow it. For example, if the president sets a goal to balance the budget, the council may suggest decreasing military spending. The president, however, might reject their advice if he has made promises to increase military spending.

Despite disagreements on some points, economists have been successful in describing, analyzing, and explaining economic activity. Because of this, they have helped the American people understand how the economy works.

Economists know enough today that they can prevent another severe depression. Although minor recessions are still unavoidable, economists can create policies that stimulate growth, help disadvantaged groups, and make the U.S. economy generally stronger.

Section Wrap-up

Answer these questions to check your understanding of the entire section.

1. How does the decision-making process involved in setting monetary policies differ from the decision making involved in setting fiscal policies?

_____

_____

_____

2. What is the main reason why economists' recommendations change over time?

_____

_____

_____

Expository Writing

Suppose you live in a time period when natural resources, such as fossil fuels and even water, are scarce and fluctuations in their prices greatly disrupt the economy. How might that affect the type fiscal policies enacted and the means in which the policies are enacted?

_____

_____

_____

_____

_____

_____

_____

_____

_____

_____

_____

Absolute and Comparative Advantage

Big Idea

As you read pages 441–445 in your textbook, complete this graphic organizer by defining each term and providing an example of each.

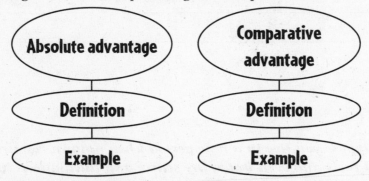

 **Notes** | **Read to Learn**

Why Nations Trade (page 442)

Synthesizing Information

As you read, complete the sentence below.

_____

are goods which a nation specializes in producing, while _____ are not.

Why do nations trade? Because they believe that the goods they receive are worth more than they give up. Often nations specialize, which means they focus on making the goods they produce the best. Nations then trade their goods for others that are more expensive or even impossible for them to produce. Honduras specializes in bananas, for example, and the Middle East specializes in oil. Both nations trade the goods in which they specialize. States and regions also specialize. For example, the soil near Tyler, Texas, produces beautiful roses. Tyler has a long history of selling roses to flower shops across the country.

You can learn about a nation's economy by studying what goods it imports and exports. **Exports** are goods and services that a nation sells to others. A nation's exports tell you about the goods that it does produce efficiently. **Imports** are the goods and services that a nation buys from other nations. A nation's imports tell you which goods it does not produce efficiently.

International trade is important to all countries. Most trade is in goods, but trade in services is growing. Services include insurance and banking. The United States imports both goods and services. It has a huge volume of trade with other nations.

Notes | Read to Learn

The Basis for Trade (page 443)

Comparing and Contrasting

How are the concepts of a comparative advantage and an absolute advantage similar?

_____

_____

How are they different?

_____

_____

Drawing Conclusions

As you read, complete the sentence below.

If the countries Alpha and Beta both have the natural resource oil, but it is easier for Alpha to drill for it and pump it, _____ would have the

_____

advantage.

Nations benefit the most from trade when they specialize. For every country, some products can be bought more cheaply from other countries than can be made in that country. Absolute advantage and comparative advantage explain why this is true.

Absolute advantage is a country's ability to produce more of a given product than another country. Absolute advantage occurs because of many factors, such as the availability of natural resources, climate, and soil quality. Having an absolute advantage enables a country to produce enough of a product to consume some and export some.

When comparing the absolute advantage that a nation has over another nation for a particular product, economists use a **production possibilities frontier.** It is a diagram that shows the maximum combination of goods and services an economy can produce when all resources are fully employed.

Two countries can benefit from trade even if one has a smaller output than the other. In some instances, a smaller country can produce an item more efficiently, even if it cannot produce as large a volume as a larger country. This is a **comparative advantage**—a country's ability to produce a given product *relatively* more efficiently than another country by producing it at a lower opportunity cost. **Opportunity cost** is the cost of the next-best alternative use of money, time, or resources when making a choice. Suppose the countries Alpha and Beta use all of their resources to produce two items. The country of Alpha can produce five million pounds of pineapple and one million pounds of sugarcane while the country Beta can produce two million pounds of pineapple and one million pounds of sugarcane. Compare Alpha and Beta's opportunity cost of producing sugarcane: Alpha must give up producing five pounds of pineapple for each pound of sugarcane it produces, while Beta only gives up producing two pounds of pineapple for each pound of sugarcane. Beta has a comparative advantage when producing sugarcane while Alpha has a comparative advantage when producing pineapple.

A comparative advantage is what allows both a smaller country and a larger country to benefit when trading goods. Comparative advantage applies to individuals, companies, regions, and states, as well as to nations. As countries specialize, world output increases and the world allocates resources more efficiently.

Section Wrap-up

Answer these questions to check your understanding of the entire section.

1. Why do regions, states, and nations specialize?

_____

_____

_____

2. How do smaller countries benefit from having a comparative advantage?

_____

_____

_____

Some of Brazil's imports include oil, pharmaceuticals, fertilizer, electronics, cars, and telecommunications equipment. Some of Brazil's exports include wood and wood products, coffee, gold, shoes, aluminum, vehicles, tires, and aircraft. Write an essay describing Brazil's economy by making inferences about the goods it imports and the goods it exports.

_____

_____

_____

_____

_____

_____

_____

_____

_____

_____

_____

_____

Barriers to International Trade

Big Idea

As you read pages 447–454 in your textbook, complete this graphic organizer by describing the arguments of protectionists and free traders.

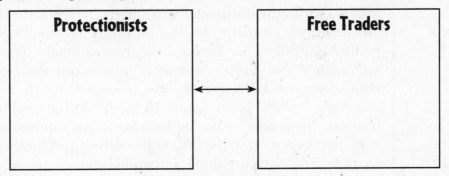

Protectionists	Free Traders

Notes | Read to Learn

Restricting International Trade (page 448)

Predicting

1. What might happen if a government did not impose a protective tariff on steel products?

_____

_____

2. How would car manufacturers be affected?

_____

_____

Governments restrict trade to protect industries. One common way to restrict trade is through a **tariff**—a tax placed on imports to increase their price in the domestic market.

One kind of tariff is a **protective tariff**, or tax designed to protect less-efficient domestic producers by raising the price of goods produced overseas. As a result, tariffs protect domestic producers from competing with foreign businesses for sales because their goods are less expensive.

The other type of tariff is a **revenue tariff**, which generates revenue for a government without prohibiting imports. Historically, the U.S. government has raised at least half of its revenue through revenue tariffs. In 1913, the government established a more profitable revenue source—the federal income tax.

Governments also restrict trade by setting quotas. This is a limit on the amount of a good that is allowed into a country. **Quotas** successfully protect domestic businesses and jobs even when high tariffs do not.

Other barriers to trade include health inspections and import licenses. Nationalism and culture influence both of these.

Arguments for Protection (page 450)

Making Generalizations

Who is hurt the most by overly protectionist policies?

_____

_____

What is the best way to protect a country's independence, industries, and workers? People have debated this question for decades. **Protectionists** are people who want to protect domestic producers against foreign competition with tariffs, quotas, and other trade barriers. **Free traders,** on the other hand, favor fewer or even no trade restrictions.

When these two groups debate, protectionists usually focus on six arguments. The first argument for trade barriers is to prevent a country from becoming too dependent on trade. The second is the **infant industries argument,** which states that new and emerging industries should be protected from foreign competition until they are strong enough to compete. The third argument is that tariffs and quotas protect domestic jobs from going overseas to cheaper foreign labor. The fourth argument is that trade barriers keep American money in the country. The fifth argument centers on the **balance of payments**—the difference between money paid to, and received from, other nations in trade. The sixth argument is national pride.

The Free Trade Movement (page 453)

Analyzing Information

What steps have been taken to make international trade easier?

1. _____

_____

2. _____

_____

3. _____

_____

4. _____

_____

During the Great Depression, restrictive tariffs set around the world almost stopped trade completely. This showed that high tariffs could hurt more then they helped. In 1934, the United States passed the Reciprocal Trade Agreements Act. The act included the **most favored nation clause.** This is a trade law that gives a country the same tariff reduction that the United States gives to any third country.

In 1947, 23 countries signed the General Agreement on Tariffs and Trade (GATT). The GATT was later replaced by the **World Trade Organization** (WTO). The WTO is an international agency that administers trade agreements, settles trade disputes between governments, organizes trade negotiations, and provides technical assistance and training for developing countries. The GATT and WTO have lowered tariffs and quotas around the world, and international trade is booming.

In 1993, Canada, Mexico, and the United States signed the **North American Free Trade Agreement** (NAFTA), which reduced tariffs and increased trade among the three nations. Although some American workers lost their jobs, free trade among the NAFTA partners has helped the countries to capitalize on their comparative advantages.

Section Wrap-up

Answer these questions to check your understanding of the entire section.

1. What are quotas, and what are their benefits?

_____

_____

_____

2. What is NAFTA, and how has it affected the countries involved?

_____

_____

_____

Descriptive Writing

Write two short letters. Write one from the perspective of a shopper newly able to buy foreign goods at competitive prices. Write the second letter from the perspective of a factory worker learning that he or she will lose his or her job when the plant moves to another country.

_____

_____

_____

_____

_____

_____

_____

_____

_____

_____

Foreign Exchange and Trade Deficits

Big Idea

As you read pages 456–461 in your textbook, complete this graphic organizer by describing the effects of a long-lasting trade deficit.

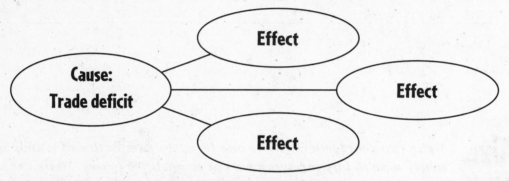

 **Notes**

Read to Learn

Financing International Trade *(page 457)*

Drawing Conclusions

Why do you think that the foreign exchange rate is expressed in terms of U.S. dollars and in terms of foreign currencies?

_____

_____

_____

In international finance, different currencies are bought and sold. These currencies are known as **foreign exchange.**

The **foreign exchange rate** is the price of one country's currency in terms of another country's currency. This rate is reported both in terms of the U. S. dollar equivalent and in terms of foreign currency units per U. S. dollar.

For most of the 1900s, people used a **fixed exchange rate.** Under this system, the price of one currency is fixed in terms of another currency so that the rate does not change. The fixed exchange rate worked well when the world was on a gold standard. The gold standard allowed people to easily compare the value of currencies, which tended to keep exchange rates fair.

When the United States switched to **flexible exchange rates** (also known as **floating exchange rates**) in 1971, the world followed. Under this system, the forces of supply and demand establish the value of international currencies. This system has worked fairly well. The switch to flexible rates, for instance, did not interrupt the growth of international trade, as many people feared it would.

Notes

Read to Learn

Trade Deficits and Surpluses (page 460)

(page 460)

Formulating Questions

Before you read about trade deficits and surpluses, write two questions you think will be answered by the passage.

1. _____

_____

2. _____

_____

Determining Cause and Effect

1. How does a continuing trade surplus affect the value of the dollar?

_____

_____

_____

_____

A country has a **trade deficit** whenever the value of its imports exceeds the value of its exports. It has a **trade surplus** whenever the value of its exports exceeds the value of its imports. The value of the goods depends on the international value of the country's currency.

The Fed has tracked the value of the dollar since the dollar started to float in 1971. In determining the **trade-weighted value of the dollar,** the Fed measures the dollar's strength against a group of major foreign currencies. When this index falls, the dollar is weak compared to other countries. When the index rises, the dollar is strong. When the dollar rises, foreign goods become less expensive and American exports more expensive. Imports rise, exports fall, and trade deficit results. With more dollars going abroad, the value of the dollar falls.

A persistent trade imbalance can affect income and employment. As the value of the dollar falls, imports become more expensive and exports more affordable for foreigners. This imbalance benefits American export industries, but makes it difficult for American import industries.

Since the value of the dollar changes daily, what is better for the nation—a strong dollar or a weak dollar? The answer is neither. Trade deficits tend to correct themselves automatically according to the price system at work under flexible exchange rates. A strong currency leads to a deficit in the balance of payments. This leads to a decline in the value of the currency. A weak currency generally causes a trade surplus, which eventually pulls up the value of the currency.

These changes mean that one sector of the American economy benefits while another is hurt. There is no net gain in having either a strong or a weak dollar. As a result, the United States and many other nations no longer create economic policies solely intended to improve the strength of their currency.

Section Wrap-up

Answer these questions to check your understanding of the entire section.

1. How does the foreign exchange market help trade?

_____

_____

_____

2. Why does the Fed track the value of the dollar relative to foreign currencies?

_____

_____

_____

Expository Writing

Suppose you own a fabric company in the United States. A trade journal forecasts that the tariffs on fabrics imported from China and India will be reduced next year. Write a cause and effect essay describing how the decrease in tariffs will affect the sales of your fabric and what steps you would take to prevent the negative affects.

_____

_____

_____

_____

_____

_____

_____

_____

_____

_____

_____

_____

Economic Development

Big Idea

As you read pages 469–477 in your textbook, complete this graphic organizer by identifying at least two reasons why it would probably be more difficult to bring about change in a traditional economic system than in a market economy.

The difficulty of change in a traditional economy	

 **Notes** | **Read to Learn**

The Importance of Economic Development (page 470)

Predicting

Will industrialized nations be more or less motivated to help developed nations as the trade of goods and services between nations increases?

_____

_____

_____

Poverty is an economic and political problem that greatly affects people living in developing countries as well as industrialized nations. A **developing country** has a relatively low average per capita income and a less developed infrastructure, education, and health care system compared to industrialized countries. In order to compare the level of poverty between nations, economists first convert each nation's GNP to a common currency. Then, they find the per capita GNP to account for the varying population between nations.

Economic growth is the most effective way to reduce poverty. Economic growth, especially in developing countries, has caused poverty around the world to decline since 1981.

Industrialized nations have humanitarian, economic, and political motivations to assist developing countries. Some people in industrialized nations believe it is a moral responsibility to help them. Economic considerations include that developing countries provide natural resources and markets for industrial nations. A political consideration is that developed countries with a strong market economy are more stable.

 **Notes** | **Read to Learn**

Stages of Economic Development (page 472)

Analyzing Information

Identify the stage of economic development associated with each characteristic:

1. Mature service sector

_____

2. Per capita income begins to increase

_____

Some economists believe that developing countries pass through standard stages of economic development. During the first stage, **primitive equilibrium,** a country's economy is stagnant, and economic decision-making is determined by culture and tradition. The second stage of economic development, transition, marks the beginnings of economic change when people begin to question old customs. The third stage of development is **takeoff.** It occurs after barriers of primitive equilibrium are overcome. In this stage, agricultural productivity improves, new industries begin to grow, and the country begins to save and invest its national income.

The fourth stage, semidevelopment, is defined by the increase of per capita income and the growth of core industries. By the time a nation reaches the final stage, high development, the economy is able to satisfy basic needs and wants. Service and manufacturing sectors mature, while industrial production becomes less important.

Obstacles to Development (page 474)

Synthesizing Information

As you read, complete the following sentence.

If developing countries aim for zero population growth, as the GNP increases so will the _____

_____.

Many countries face significant challenges to economic development. Limited natural resources and restricted opportunities for trade prevent economic growth. So can disease—in people as well as livestock—and drug addiction. Low literacy and technical skills are also significant obstacles.

Another obstacle is high population growth. The combination of a high **crude birthrate,** or number of live births per 1,000 people, and an increasing **life expectancy** makes it difficult for developing countries to increase per capita GNP. Some economists believe that developed societies should seek **zero population growth,** or the condition in which the average number of births and deaths balance.

A nation's financial decisions and money supply can create obstacles. **External debt**—the borrowed money that a country owes to foreign countries and banks—is a major problem for developing nations. Some nations consider **defaulting,** or not repaying borrowed money, at the risk of not being able to borrow again. **Capital flight,** the legal or illegal export of a nation's currency and foreign exchange, is another obstacle to economic development. Capital flight limits the funds available for domestic capital investment.

An unstable political climate also prevents economic development, including government corruption. The long lasting effects of war in developing countries also prevent development.

Section Wrap-up

Answer these questions to check your understanding of the entire section.

1. Why do economists use the per capita GNP to compare nations' economies?

_____

_____

_____

2. What is the most important characteristic of the takeoff stage?

_____

_____

_____

Persuasive Writing

From the perspective of a non-profit leader in the United States, write a letter asking people to donate money to reduce poverty in developing countries. Choose either moral, economic, or political arguments.

_____

_____

_____

_____

_____

_____

_____

_____

_____

_____

_____

_____

Achieving Economic Development

Big Idea

As you read pages 479–484 in your textbook, complete this graphic organizer by describing the ways developing countries can finance economic development.

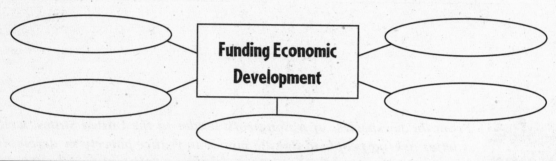

Funding Economic Development

 **Notes**   **Read to Learn**

Funding Economic Development (page 480)

Analyzing Information

How do grants from foreign governments differ from loans from international agencies?

_____

_____

_____

_____

Economic development requires funding from internal or external sources. In a market economy, internal funds are generated by savings. In a command economy, the government can force saving by requiring people to work.

Micro loans are a very successful source of funding in developing countries. Micro loans are small, unsecured loans made primarily to women to generate income.

External sources of funding include international agencies, foreign governments, and private investment. The **International Monetary Fund** offers advice and financial assistance, while the **World Bank** makes loans and provides financial assistance and advice. One agency of the World Bank offers **soft loans** that may never be paid back to very needy countries. Foreign governments are another source of external funding; however, government grants are often given to promote political goals rather than to aid the neediest countries.

Foreign investors provide private capital to develop profitable industries in developing countries. However, many investors are discouraged by **expropriation**—government confiscation.

Read to Learn

Regional Economic Cooperation *(page 483)*

Problems and Solutions

1. What problems faced by smaller countries, such as Italy, are solved by regional trade agreements, such as the EU?

_____

_____

_____

_____

2. How do regional agreements solve the problems?

_____

_____

_____

_____

_____

_____

_____

Nations engage in regional economic agreements to foster economic growth among member nations. Types of regional economic agreements include free-trade areas and customs unions. A **free-trade area** is a group of countries that have agreed to reduce trade barriers among themselves, but lack a common tariff barrier for nonmembers. A **customs union** is a group of countries that have agreed to reduce trade barriers among themselves and have uniform tariffs for nonmembers.

The **European Union (EU)** is a successful example of regional cooperation. The EU is an economic, political, and social union established in 1993 by the Maastricht Treaty. It was the successor of the European Community, a customs union. The EU is the largest single unified market in terms of population and output and the world. It does not have any internal barriers regulating the flow of workers, financial capital, or goods and services. Citizens of member nations have EU passports. Many member nations share a single currency, the **euro,** introduced in January 2002.

Other countries have also created regional agreements. For example, **ASEAN** is a group of 10 Southeast Asian nations working to promote regional cooperation, economic growth, and trade.

Countries that produce the same goods can make economic agreements as well. A **cartel,** for example, is a group of sellers or producers acting together to raise prices by restricting the availability of a product. In 1960, several oil-producing nations formed the Organization of Petroleum Exporting Countries (OPEC), a cartel with the purpose of driving economic development by inflating oil prices. Although OPEC's efforts have directed trillions of dollars away from industrialized countries to OPEC member countries, corruption, war, and other factors have prevented OPEC member countries from rapidly developing.

Section Wrap-up

Answer these questions to check your understanding of the entire section.

1. What type of funding is particularly limited in a command economy? Explain.

_____

_____

_____

2. How is a cartel different from a customs union?

_____

_____

_____

Expository Writing

From the perspective of an applicant for a micro loan, write a letter explaining why you are a good applicant for the program and how you will use the loan to generate income. Remember that micro loans are usually for very small amounts.

_____

_____

_____

_____

_____

_____

_____

_____

_____

_____

_____

_____

The Transition to Capitalism

Big Idea

As you read pages 486–495 in your textbook, complete this graphic organizer by selecting a country and describing how it is making the transition to capitalism.

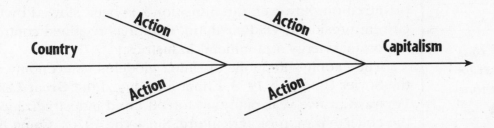

Country — Action — Action — Capitalism
Action — Action

Notes | **Read to Learn**

Problems of Transition *(page 487)*

Problems and Solutions

What problem do vouchers solve?

_____

_____

_____

_____

Capitalism, the economic system in which private citizens own and use the factors of production to make a profit, is the most efficient way to organize large economies. Many countries have transitioned to capitalist economies because capitalism provides a greater standard of living.

The transition to capitalism requires privatization of property and industry, a change in political power, new policies, and new incentives. **Privatization** is the conversion of state-owned factories and other property to private ownership. Some countries used **vouchers,** or certificates that could be used to purchase government owned property during privatization, to aid in the distribution of property. The transition from communism to capitalism also requires that leaders in old governments give up political power in order to provide opportunities for entrepreneurs and capitalists. The shift further demands that countries develop safety nets to protect citizens from the instability and costs of capitalism. Finally, people have to come to understand profit incentives as well as learn a new set of skills, such as how to make economic decisions on their own.

Notes | Read to Learn

Countries and Regions in Transition *(page 489)*

Comparing and Contrasting

List two ways that China's transition to capitalism was similar to Russia's.

1. _____

_____

2. _____

_____

List two ways that China's transition was different than Russia's.

3. _____

_____

4. _____

_____

The transition to capitalism has gone more smoothly for some countries than others. In Russia, political leaders have had a great effect. During the Soviet era, the government controlled economic activity with **Five-Year Plans,** or economic plans used to coordinate the development of industry and agriculture. The **Gosplan**—the central authority of the Five-Year plans—introduced **collectivization.** It forced common ownership of all agricultural, industrial, and trading enterprises. After central planning failed, a government led by President Mikael Gorbachev introduced **perestroika,** the first step towards capitalism. His successor, Boris Yeltsin used vouchers to accelerate privatization; however, the transition has been slowed by the current president, Vladmir Putin. Putin has regained control of important energy and mineral industries.

The People's Republic of China modeled its economy after the Soviet Union. In 1958, China introduced the **Great Leap Forward,** a five-year plan that forced rapid industrialization and the collectivization of agriculture. Since the 1970s, China has achieved substantial economic growth by gradually moving towards capitalism. Today, China is a major economic power.

Many countries in Eastern Europe rapidly embraced capitalism. Poland's transition began with an independent Polish labor union founded in 1980 by Lech Walesa, called **Solidarity.** Hungary's historically strong **black market,** or a market in which goods are sold illegally, eased that country's transition.

Other Faces of Capitalism *(page 492)*

Making Inferences

Why might Japan develop capital intensive production methods?

_____

_____

_____

_____

Capitalist economies differ. Technology has contributed greatly to the success of Japan's capitalist economy. Japan relies on **capital-intensive** production methods, such as robotics. Most large Japanese firms, however, belong to a **keiretsu,** a group of firms governed by a board which regulates competition. This practice slows economic growth. South Korea is another success story of capitalism. South Korea has grown from one of the poorest nations with the highest **population density** in the world to a well-developed industrial economy. Taiwan is a real economic power in Asia. Government planning has been the key to its success in the past. Another capitalist country is Singapore; its government incentives have attracted multinational corporations and stimulated growth. Sweden's form of capitalism, which transitioned from socialism, combines high-tech capitalism and liberal welfare benefits.

Section Wrap-up

Answer these questions to check your understanding of the entire section.

1. Explain how black markets helped Hungary overcome one or more specific problems faced by economies in transition.

_____

_____

_____

2. What is the difference between privatization and collectivization?

_____

_____

_____

Descriptive Writing

Suppose you are a mother or father of three, living in a country in transition from communism to capitalism. Write a descriptive letter to a relative explaining how your daily life has changed.

_____

_____

_____

_____

_____

_____

_____

_____

_____

_____

_____

_____

Globalization: Characteristics and Trends

Big Idea

As you read pages 501–507 in your textbook, complete this graphic organizer by explaining how globalization affects products and countries.

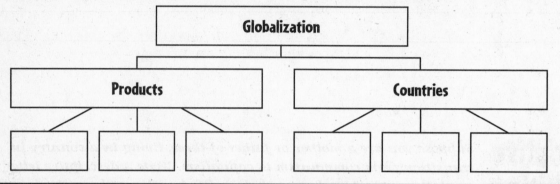

 **Notes**   **Read to Learn**

Characteristics of Globalization *(page 502)*

Distinguishing Fact from Opinion

Is the following statement from the passage a fact or an opinion?
"Americans do not need to worry."

_____

_____

Globalization is the movement toward a more integrated and interdependent world economy. **Multinationals** are corporations whose business activities take place in many different countries.

Some multinationals move or build production facilities closer to customers or to cheaper sources of labor and raw materials. Modern production, communications, data processing, and shipping technologies make global manufacturing possible. Another trend of globalization is **outsourcing**—hiring outside firms to complete some tasks at a lower cost. This trend is controversial because many Americans fear losing their jobs.

Globalization has also resulted in the growth of international bodies that promote trade. Examples include the **General Agreement on Tariffs and Trade (GATT),** an agreement which extended tariff privileges and reduced import quotas; the World Trade Organization (WTO), which resolves trade conflicts; the International Monetary Fund (IMF), which offers advice and aid to ensure the acceptance of a country's; and the World Bank, which helps developing countries join global markets. The United Nations helps to preserve peace among nations.

Globalization Trends (page 504)

Drawing Conclusions

As you read, underline the sentence that supports the following conclusion.

Fear of interdependence is a reason why many people support energy independence in the United States.

Analyzing Information

What issues does regional economic integration address?

1. _____

_____

2. _____

_____

3. _____

_____

Two important trends of globalization are growing economic interdependence among nations and growing regional integration. Specialization by producers and the division of labor has lead to increased productivity. A **division of labor** is the separation of work into a number of individual tasks performed by different workers. A firm that employs these methods may have a **comparative advantage,** meaning it produces the same goods more efficiently than other firms. This would make the firm more competitive. In a global context, countries that are best at using capital and technology efficiently are the ones that manufacture important products. Then they can exchange the products for other nations' raw materials. The result is global interdependence. Generally, all nations benefit, however, there is cause for concern. A breakdown anywhere in the exchange of goods could affect all nations as well.

To ease the way for increased interdependence, nations in different parts of the world have pursued regional economic integration. The European Union (EU) is furthest along this path. The EU began as the **European Coal and Steel Community (ECSC),** a group of six European countries formed in 1951 to coordinate iron and steel production to ensure peace among members. Today there are 25 member nations, about half of which have adopted the euro as their currency. Most internal barriers to the movement of workers, financial capital, goods, and services have been removed.

The EU's economic growth and political stability has led to other regional integration efforts, including the Association for Southeast Asian Nations (ASEAN), the Common Market for Eastern and Southern Africa (COMESA), and the **Free Trade Area of the Americas (FTAA).** The FTAA is a 34-nation group established in 1994 in order to set up a regional free trade area in the Americas with no internal barriers to trade. In the future, different regional groups may form even larger global markets. Since economic cooperation usually leads to more political cooperation, globalization may someday lead to economic growth and political stability among all countries.

Globalization has and will continue to encounter resistance. Conflicts arise from groups and individual's fears of losing jobs, industries, and ways of life. Politics can also interfere, such as when disagreements keep nations from cooperating economically. Finally, some groups are opposed to capitalism in general and so they oppose its spread through globalization.

Section Wrap-up

Answer these questions to check your understanding of the entire section.

1. What effect has globalization had on organizations, such as the WTO, the IMF, and the World Bank? Why?

_____

_____

_____

2. How are the concepts of regional integration, economic growth, and political stability related?

_____

_____

_____

Expository Writing

From the point of view of a protectionist, a person who is against free-trade, write a cause and effect essay that describes the potential problems of globalization.

_____

_____

_____

_____

_____

_____

_____

_____

_____

_____

_____

_____

Chapter 18, Section 2 (Pages 509–518)

Global Problems and Economic Incentives

Big Idea

As you read pages 509–518 in your textbook, complete this graphic organizer by identifying and describing the global problems that scarcity can bring.

Problem	Description

Notes | **Read to Learn**

Global Population Growth (page 510)

Comparing and Contrasting

As you read, complete the following sentence.

Malthus's prediction about population growth has proven to be more accurate in the

_____

countries than in the

_____

countries.

The basic economic problem on a local and global scale is **scarcity**—the ability to meet people's unlimited wants with limited resources. In 1798 the economist Thomas Malthus thought that the world population would grow faster than the earth's ability to feed it. Eventually this would result in people around the world living in a state of **subsistence**—when a society produces only enough to support itself. This prediction is already a reality in many developing countries, where poverty is widespread. However, the world's population growth rate seems to be slowing. In fact, the rate has decreased every year since 1963. Industrialized nations have the lowest rates of population growth, while poorer developing nations usually have the highest rates. Malthus did not foresee how advances in productivity would reduce scarcity or that people would choose to have fewer children.

Economic incentives affect population growth. In an industrialized country, children cost a lot of money to raise. By having fewer children, a family reduces these costs. But in the developing world, each child is seen as a worker, so parents have many children.

Chapter 18, Section 2

157

Read to Learn

The Demand for Resources *(page 512)*

Synthesizing Information

As you read, complete the following sentence.

When oil prices are
_____

people will conserve energy, and they will
_____

when oil prices are
_____.

Population growth increases the scarcity of resources. Economists recognize two general types. A **renewable resource** is a natural resource that can be replenished. For example, **hydropower**—power or energy generated by moving water—is the most commonly used of this type. **Biomass,** another example, is energy made from wood, peat, municipal solid waste, straw, corn, tires, landfill gases, fish oils, and other waste. Ethanol is a biomass. It is used in **gasohol**—a fuel composed of 90 percent unleaded gasoline and 10 percent ethanol. Other examples are solar power and wind-generated electricity.

Most of our energy comes from **nonrenewable resources**—resources that cannot be replenished. The major category of this type is fossil fuels which may last only a few more generations. Oil is the most popular nonrenewable energy source, followed by natural gas, coal, and nuclear energy.

Measures meant to limit individuals' energy use have generally failed. People respond more to market and price incentives. For example, in 1981, there was a worldwide oil **glut**—a substantial oversupply. The resulting low oil prices lessen the incentive to search for alternative energy sources and exploration for new oil sources. Consumers bought large houses and low-mileage SUVs. Then in 2006 energy prices rose again, leading to a renewed interest in developing alternative fuels.

Pollution and Economic Incentives *(page 516)*

Identifying the Main Idea

Underline the sentence that gives the most important idea of this passage.

Legislation, fees, and permits can help solve the global problem of **pollution**—the contamination of air, water, or soil by the discharge of a poisonous or noxious substance. Society must find ways to eliminate reasons to pollute because of harmful effects, such as acid rain that falls over North America. **Acid rain** is a mixture of rainwater and sulfur dioxide.

In the United States, legislated standards have been effective in limiting air, water, and auto emissions. The government has used fees to limit pollution. By taxing polluting firms, they have an incentive to clean up or stop the pollution if it costs less. The Environmental Protection Agency (EPA) has also used **pollution permits**—federal permits allowing a public utility to pollute the air. Suppose a coal-burning utility buys a right to pollute for $400 per ton, but it only costs $350 to stop polluting, it will stop and sell the permit to a utility that has higher expenses. In successive years, the permits become more costly and scarce, increasing the incentive to stop polluting.

Answer these questions to check your understanding of the entire section.

1. Why is Malthus's population prediction a reality in developing nations?

_____

_____

_____

2. Why do price incentives result in the conservation of natural resources?

_____

_____

_____

Descriptive Writing

Suppose you lived near a coal-fired power plant in a developing nation. The new plant has provided your region's first reliable electricity. Write a letter to a pen pal that describes how the plant has changed your life—both positively and negatively.

_____

_____

_____

_____

_____

_____

_____

_____

_____

_____

Applying the Economic Way of Thinking

Big Idea

As you read pages 520–523 in your textbook, complete this graphic organizer by describing how capitalism helps us with economic choices.

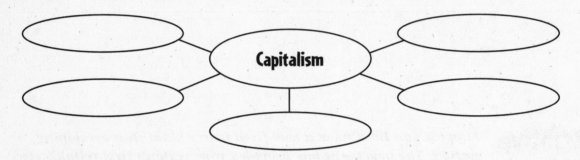

 **Notes**

Read to Learn

A Framework for Decision Making *(page 521)*

Analyzing Information

Name three reasons why it is important to study economics.

1. _____

   _____

2. _____

   _____

3. _____

   _____

By studying economics and by using economic tools, we learn to make the best economic choices. The National Council on Economic Education recommends using the following five steps to make good decisions. First, state the problem or issue. Next decide upon the personal or broad social goals to be met. Think about various effective methods of achieving the goals. Then, select the economic ideas you need to know to understand the problem, and use them as a framework to evaluate the various methods. Finally, decide which method will help you attain the most goals or the most important goals.

Economists use different tools to help them solve problems. Marginal analysis is one of the most important decision-making tools. Firms use it when they make a decision to produce more output. If the extra benefits outweigh the extra costs of production, the firm decides to produce more. This process is a **cost-benefit analysis,** which compares the cost of an action to its benefits.

When it comes to cost, we must remember that economists refer to **opportunity cost**—cost of the next best alternative use of money, time, or resources when making a choice. Opportunity costs more than just monetary costs.

Read to Learn

Coping With the Future *(page 522)*

Problems and Solutions

What problems from its laissez-faire beginnings has modern-day capitalism solved?

_____

_____

_____

_____

Making Inferences

How will our modified free enterprise system react to an increase of multinationals and trade?

_____

_____

_____

_____

Our understanding of how our capitalist system works helps us to make good economic decisions. As you learned, the United States has a **modified free enterprise system** or a free enterprise economy with some government involvement. This means that buyers and sellers are free to make all their own economic decisions in order to meet their wants and needs. The free interaction of the forces of supply and demand establishes market prices. In turn, changes in prices send signals to producers and consumers as to whether or not they should make different economic choices. In short, the market forces of supply and demand indicate to producers and consumers how to reallocate resources when the economy changes.

Although communist and socialist systems once existed in many parts of the world, capitalism is now the globe's dominant economic system. However, capitalism has changed from its early laissez-faire days because people have addressed some of the weaknesses that Karl Marx and others identified years ago. For example, early capitalism did not provide economic cushions for the elderly, the ill, or the incapacitated. In order to create a fair and more just society, most capitalist economies have altered their systems. This includes the United States. Our free-market economy, based on capitalism, has been modified to satisfy the economic goals of freedom, efficiency, equity, security, full employment, price stability, and economic growth.

In general, capitalism adjusts to change just the way a market adjusts to small changes in supply and demand. That is, it changes gradually. The adjustments are so small that they are hard to notice in the short run. Capitalism's ability to change, grow, and adapt ensures its future success.

Section Wrap-up

Answer these questions to check your understanding of the entire section.

1. What resources are considered when weighing the opportunity cost of an economic decision?

_____

_____

_____

2. What has influenced changes made to our economic system?

_____

_____

_____

Expository Writing

Use the National Council on Economic Education's five steps to useful decision making to show how you could solve an economic problem that you might face in your own life.

_____

_____

_____

_____

_____

_____

_____

_____

_____

_____

_____